Cover: Salisbury Cathedral on the occasion of King George V's Silver Jubilee, 1935. Photograph by the author, using a five-minute exposure with a box Brownie camera.

This engraving has been taken from William Dodsworth's "An Historical Account of the Episcopal See and Cathedral Church of Sarum or Salisbury", printed in 1814 by Brodie and Dowding, New Canal, proprietors of the Salisbury and Winchester Journal.

UNDER SALISBURY SPIRE

*Memories
from the
late Twenties
to the first
year of
World War II*

by

Arthur Maidment

**A
Salisbury Journal
Publication**

First published 1993 by:

Salisbury Journal
Rollestone House
8-12 Rollestone Street
Salisbury
Wiltshire

Edited by Jennie Levin

ISBN 0 9513920 3 4

ACKNOWLEDGEMENTS

THE author wishes to thank the following for help so willingly given:
my son, Gordon and daughter, Pamela, Mrs Dee Adcock, Mr and Mrs
Robert Newman, Sqd Ldr Bernard Noble RAF (Rtd), Mr David
Sanders, Mr Wilson Sanders, Miss Pamela Street, well known Wiltshire
authoress, for her kind review on the back cover, Mr Jimmy Thompson,
Mr Leslie Tolley, Mr D. G. Upward (Southampton Hall of Aviation), Mr
Gareth Weekes (Bournemouth Evening Echo), Mr and Mrs D. S. Woods,
and Mr Ray McEnhill, who has helped make this book possible.
    Thanks are also due to the following for allowing the use of
photographs from their collections; Mr Peter Daniels (photos on Pages
21, 35, 48, 60, 79, 130, 144, 150, and 155), Mr J. P. Daalhuizen of
Debenhams (Page 134), Mr Graham Dilks of the Odeon, Salisbury
(Page 74), Mr Alan Richardson (Pages 26, 74, 144 and 150),
Southampton Hall of Aviation (Page 48), The Battle of Britain
International Library (Page 188).

CONTENTS

This sequel to my earlier book, *I Remember, I Remember* * is
dedicated to the many kind people who have given me
encouragement to continue writing my reminiscences.
Under Salisbury Spire deals with the years between 1926 and 1940.

It was the wish of my late wife, Madge, that I should record my
memories. I little thought when I started the task in 1989 that two
volumes would be needed to cover the first third of my life, but
they were indeed eventful years.

Now at the age of 77, it is my hope that I can finish the job of
telling the story of my lifetime, covering as it does, the major part
of the twentieth century. I do not claim that my days have been
very different to millions of my contemporaries,
I'm just "a man in the street".

Arthur Meadment

**A book of the same title, which I read several times when a small
boy, was written by Mrs Marshall and published in 1890.*

PROLOGUE

(being Chapter Twenty-five of "I Remember — I Remember")

Easter 1926 was quite a significant time for me. Firstly I was due to go up into Standard Six to be taught by the rather frightening Sammy Edwards. During the previous two years, I had been in Mr Ralph Shergold's class. To be taught by the same teacher for two successive years was a unique occurrence and only came about because the previous Easter Mr Windust had taken up the headship of a boys' school at Weymouth. Sammy Edwards moved up to take Windy's classes and Ralph Shergold moved up from Standard Four to Five. A new master, Mr Simmonds, a fine athlete, came to take over Standard Four. Those two years spent under Ralph had been extremely happy so I was saddened to leave him.

Secondly, in March I had taken the first two parts of the Grammar School Entrance Examinations (later to become the 11-plus). They were held at our school over two successive days; on the first morning we had Mathematics, Part I and the afternoon was taken up with English Part I. On the next day we had the second part of both subjects. The examination was compulsory for all reaching the age of eleven between September 1925 and August 1926.

When the results came through, while I was pleased to head the list with an overall 90%, 216 marks from 240, my reaction was somewhat muted for I was not sure that I wished to go on to Bishop Wordsworth's School. Dad and Mum wanted me to take the scholarship exams, to be held at the end of May, as both my elder sisters had won places in their turn and, though neither parent put pressure on me, I was well aware of what was expected.

When we started the new term, I soon discovered that Sammy Edwards was exactly as everyone had warned — a good teacher but given to bursts of violent temper. Only some five feet seven inches tall, he was a real Jekyll and Hyde character, going from charm one moment to raging outburst the next.

When I arrived in Standard Six, I was only eleven and a half$\frac{1}{2}$ years of age and, as he took both Six and Seven, I had, if I stayed at St Martins' until school leaving age, to look forward to almost three years under his tutelage.

It was precisely this thought that made up my mind about the Bishop's School. One Thursday morning, towards the end of April, the final lesson was taken up making pencil drawings of a wooden box which had the lid raised to reveal three compartments inside. It was a good exercise in perspective, I was quite pleased with my outline drawing and had just started shading when suddenly I received a terrific blow to my right ear. Sammy had come up behind from the back of the class and had given me a clout that left my head ringing for the rest of the lesson. He shouted: "That's not shading, that's just scribbling."

At the end of the morning, my mind was made up. I just could not countenance Sammy for three more years, so ran home and blurted out to Mum that yes, I did want to take the scholarship exam. Neither parent asked what had brought about this sudden change of heart. I told no-one and was quite proud that Sammy had not brought one tear.

The exams at Bishop Wordsworth's School were held on two successive Saturday mornings. The first was taken up with written work — maths and English, the latter including a long piece of dictation. This, taken from Robert Louis Stevenson's *Treasure Island* was made difficult, for it was read by Mr MacFarlane, the senior English master, who spoke with a pronounced Scots burr. The following Saturday was mostly written work followed by individual oral examination by Mr Reuben Bracher, the headmaster.

One evening in early July, I was playing in a House cricket match at Shady Bower, when my eldest sister, Gertrude, who had just completed her second year at Bristol University, came cycling through the gates in great excitement. A letter had just arrived to say that I had been awarded a scholarship. Everyone made a great fuss of me, while I wondered what might have happened if Sammy Edwards had not tried to knock my head off.

During that May, the country was almost brought to a standstill by the General Strike, which started on Tuesday May 4th and was called off on the 12th. It did not affect Salisbury as much as the larger towns and cities — there were few local trade unionists, with the exception of railwaymen. While most of these went on strike, some continued to work and, though there was no violence, had to pass through picket lines to the shouts of "scab". The strike started in the mining industry and Dad sympathised with them, but could not understand why the comparatively well paid railwaymen tried to hold the country to ransom.

The miners really did have a case. For several years we had seen, almost daily, the plight of men as they passed through Salisbury, making their way on foot from South Wales to Southampton in the vain hope of finding work. They would go slowly along the streets singing away (many of them had excellent voices), cap in hand hoping for a copper or two with which to buy a meal. The singing was essential if they were not to be charged with begging and though no-one had much spare cash, generally their efforts did not go unrewarded. Those who could not afford to give pennies, gave in kind, either food or a can of tea. It was a tragic sight, for some of those men, driven to despair by years of unemployment, were forced to seek work in faraway places and make the journey without money for fares or sustenance.

The summer term carried on much as usual and I was sorry as time elapsed to be leaving St Martin's and my friends, most of whom I had known for almost nine years. I knew that from the next term, I would become in their eyes a "Bishop bulldog", and that relationships would be different.

The last afternoon arrived all too quickly and, at the end of term assembly, those boys who were leaving had to line up in front of the headmaster's dais. Four of us were to go on to Bishop Wordsworth's — George Fulford and I won scholarships, Phil Mealing and Ted Haskell were to enter as fee paying pupils at two guineas, or two pounds, two shillings a term. Mr Russ went along the line, shook hands with each of us, wishing us well, then called on the school for a cheer. So my time, a happy time, at the school came to an end. Alf Norris and I took our well worn path along St Martin's Church Street across St Ann's Street into Rampart Road. I remember we were both quiet and as we reached the Milford Hill corner, stopped and stood, hardly knowing what to say. Then Alf broke the ice with: "Well, we shan't be doing this walk any more."

We wished one another "all the best", then in manly fashion made our way, Alf to his Greencroft Street home, and I slowly down the hill to turn into Culver Street as I had done for the past eight years. It was the end of an era.

Chapter One 1926/1927
Salisbury celebrates seven centuries

In the Twenties and Thirties, Salisbury enjoyed a Cricket Week, played at the South Wilts Club ground at Bemerton. It always started on the Friday prior to August Bank Holiday, which was then the first Monday of that month.

The programme followed the same pattern each year, the first two days were taken up with a game against Eton Ramblers, Bank Holiday Monday and Tuesday saw the visit of Surrey Second Eleven and the week concluded with a match against either Berkshire or Dorset. Admission was free for schoolboys (I can't say schoolchildren for I don't remember girls being present) so I usually got on my bike if the weather was fine to make the most of this cricket feast.

For some reason I was late arriving on August Monday, 1926 and missed the opening overs, but it was quite a shock to learn that Wiltshire, batting first, had already lost wickets. The reason for their problems was a young bowler playing almost his first game for Surrey. He was only eighteen years of age, was about six feet three inches in height and shaped like a beanpole. I gazed in amazement as he walked back up the slope, almost to the top boundary, before turning to make his delivery. He was so fast it was unbelievable, the Wiltshire batsmen were in real trouble, having never before faced such hostile bowling. They were all out just after lunch, the score did eventually top just over 100, with most of the runs coming after this new bowler was taken off for a rest.

He was called Alf Gover. In the years that followed he became the mainstay of Surrey's First XI bowling and played many times for England. He showed me and the Wiltshire team a new dimension to the game. One memory I have of the home side is of the complete absence of anyone from this part of the county. The captain, Col R. Awdry, his brother E.W. Awdry and R.A.C. Forrester were all solicitors from North Wilts. There was one professional, Newman — as he was paid to play, his initials were always omitted from the score cards. It was still a game played by Gentlemen and Players.

During the summer holidays of 1926, prior to my admittance into Bishop Wordsworth's School, an aunt took me on a week's visit to my uncle's home at Tottenham in London. For me this was an exciting time because during that week England regained the Ashes, which they had lost in 1912, two years before I was born. It would have been an even more memorable time if my uncle had seen fit to take me the few miles across London to the Oval, but I'm afraid he had no love for cricket. It was tantalising, I don't suppose he did it deliberately but he instead took me on a rambling tram ride right by the ground, at the time, as I learned from the next morning's paper, that my boyhood hero, Jack Hobbs, was getting a century and his opening partner, Herbert Sutcliffe, was on his way to making 161. If only I could now say truthfully in my old age: "I saw it happen — I watched cricket history being made."

My entry into the grammar school was on Tuesday, September 7th. Together with about seventy other new boys I wandered into the playground — the bell in the tiny belfry tolled and we were soon marshalled into forms. I found myself with my three other ex-St Martin's colleagues in 3i. It's a sobering thought that of those four I am the only survivor. George Fulford, who like me was a scholarship boy, died in 1986 after a crippling illness. Phil Mealing, who joined the Royal Air Force upon leaving school, was Sgt/Observer in a bomber which crashed on fields at Quidhampton in 1938, only a couple of miles from his Bemerton home, and Ted Haskell died when only in his forties.

The outstanding memory of that first morning is of the way that one of my new colleagues, a chap named Harding, seemed to be answering most of the questions put to the class. I can see him now sitting on the right hand side, halfway towards the back (there were seven rows of desks with five in each row). It was no wonder the teachers picked on him, for his hand went up a long way.

Although only thirteen, he was massive, almost a six-footer and built in proportion, always seeming to bulge on each side of the desk. Harding came from Salterton, a place foreign to me, but it was in fact a tiny hamlet near Durnford and he cycled in each day on a sit-up-and-beg bike. Strangely, I saw him some years after leaving school and he seemed to be of about the same size, whereas I had grown steadily and was then not all that much shorter.

I think the main change that I found at my new school was having a different teacher for every lesson. On the first morning we had to copy a timetable, we were then told to make another copy that evening, so that we could have one pinned to the underside of the lid of the individual desks and one in our satchels or cases. Most boys had satchels — they were much easier to carry.

At this time, in 1926, Bishop Wordsworth's School catered for boys and girls, but the sexes were segregated and almost the only time we saw any girls was on Wednesday morning — the day when the Lower School went to weekly Chapel. We sat on the right hand side and the girls were on the left, under the eagle eye of Miss Wheeler or "Pussy". She apparently earned this nickname because of her unfortunate habit of spitting as she talked — due probably to the ill-fitting dentures of that time.

During that first term, we had only one afternoon for football — the school then favoured soccer, rugby came in 1928. Each Tuesday morning half the form, names A to L, set out in a crocodile under two monitors to make their way to the gymnasium, some six hundred yards away in Brown Street. In the afternoon, the rest of the class M-Z (yes, we did have a Z, Tom Zebedee) made the same journey.

Among completely new subjects we had to tackle were Latin, French, geometry, algebra, chemistry and physics. We were taught Latin by "Fuzzy" Richards, who spent almost forty years at the school as master and then after his retirement as secretary. He was a Welshman, like me cricket-mad, and an excitable individual. French was under the guiding hand of Ma'moiselle Rambour — a lady from that country across the water who made life very difficult for us because her English was far from perfect. She was rather like an overdressed doll, always wore bright colours, make-up that was plastered on (this in the days when few ladies wore any at all) and hair that varied in colour from ginger to bright yellow.

Miss Hart, herself an old pupil, took us in history, which had been one of my favourite subjects at St Martin's, where we had covered the period from Alfred the Great in the ninth century to the Civil War in the sixteen hundreds. Now Miss Hart took us back in time to the great ages of Greece and Rome, to me it was not half so interesting but she was a good teacher.

We had various teachers for odd lessons, perhaps once a week. I remember "Dicky'" Freeman (another ex-pupil) who took us for religious knowledge, spending weeks on discussions about the catechism and the probable meaning of N or M in the following excerpt. Question: What is your name? Answer: N or M. According to Dicky this possibly meant Nicholas or Mary — the most popular names in Elizabeth's reign, when the catechism was written. I wondered all those years ago and still wonder "Does it really matter". Although Dicky was an extremely nice chap, he was not the best of teachers and would have been much better employed in handicrafts. Just before his death, I ran into him in Salisbury and he invited me to visit his home near Shaftesbury to see the silverware he had produced in retirement. He was quite a craftsman.

The two science masters were very differing characters, "Charlie" Dingle who took chemistry, seemed to me to be totally devoid of a sense of humour. His lessons were always a serious affair and I remember his total deference whenever the headmaster happened to visit the lab. I can still see Charlie making his way to school along the walk by the Close Wall in Exeter Street, from the Harnham direction. He always carried a walking stick and marched rather like a well known film comedian of that era with feet splayed (as my mother would say) at ten minutes to two o'clock, his trilby hat turned down all round the brim. Charlie sang in the Cathedral choir and was really quite a nice chap if you ever managed to get through that tough reserve. "Billy" Brewer, the physics master was a very different character. Big, with a bushy, gingery 'tache, he always brought plenty of fun into his lessons, although often the fun would be at the expense of some poor unfortunate pupil. He was, for a reason known only to himself, especially sarcastic when talking to anyone who came from Wilton, as in his opinion any natives of that borough were totally devoid of grey matter. Despite his horn-rimmed spectacles Billye was capable of some big hitting during the Masters v School cricket matches and was a good teacher. I for one certainly absorbed the principles of leverage, light and heat from him and have often found these of use in later life.

"Tommy" Smith was an excellent master — the brother-in-law of Mr Reuben Bracher, the head, he was tall, rather gaunt looking and a real disciplinarian. He taught a number of subjects but his lessons were always of interest — he had a ready fund of stories to illustrate any point and I looked forward to periods with him. He often remarked on my habit of gesticulating when talking, saying: "Maidment, have you got some French blood in you?" I have, for my great-great grandmother was indeed French.

Another good teacher was "Pimp" Warren, who took us for maths. He was short, stocky and balding, with one drawback. It was always best to keep your eye on Pimp because if he saw someone's attention was wandering then quick as a flash he would throw the chalk or occasionally the pad used for blackboard cleaning and usually the missiles found their mark. It was only by the grace of God that no serious injuries were caused.

I think one of the nicest masters was "Tarzan" Taylor who taught us for English. While his discipline left much to be desired, he was extremely kind and I still treasure the reference which he gave me when I left the school, by which time he had become my housemaster and in consequence I saw a great deal of him. Whenever I met him in later years he was always interested in my career — a wonderful chap indeed.

Last but not least was the "Old Man" — the headmaster, Mr Reuben Bracher, who had held the job since the school's foundation by Bishop John Wordsworth in 1890.

The bishop made a wonderful choice, Mr Bracher was a big man in every way, a great believer in discipline but always noted for fairness. Under his guidance the school produced many men and women who became leaders in their fields. When I entered the school he had been a member of the city council for several years and had served in the office of mayor. In the years that followed many of his former pupils also wore the mayoral chain.

On November 8th, I reached another watershed in my life when I was enrolled into the Scout troop. At that time, you carried on as a Wolf Cub until reaching the age of twelve2, which I did on September 22nd. At the next pack meeting after that day there was a special ceremony. I had to shake hands with the other members of my Cub Six, then cross the line where the members of the Scout troop were waiting to welcome me. It seemed an enormous jump — from being a king-pin, I was now a very junior tenderfoot. The unofficial initiation ceremony which I went through after parade that evening was a much worse ordeal and I am sure that the Scouts' founder, Lord Baden-Powell, would not have approved. I think the less said about this episode the better. Boys will be boys!

During the summer term of 1927 several things stand out in my memory. One is the great excitement when Colonel Lindberg made the first solo Atlantic flight from USA to France in the monoplane Spirit of St Louis. It was a talking point for a whole day — almost every lesson was devoted to discussion on the wonderful achievement.

The school's first match of the new cricket season was at Harnham Playing Field against the City Police. It was on a beautiful Saturday afternoon and I went along to watch, as Jack Harrison, who was in my class and sat in the desk immediately behind me, had been included in the school team, even though he was still well short of his fourteenth birthday. The game opened in quite sensational fashion as the police, who batted first, lost two wickets to "Fuzzy" Richards in the opening over. Fuzzy, who was cricket master, often played in games other than against school teams.

In his second over, the police batsman put up a high dolly catch to mid-off. It was Jack Harrison's catch, he was right underneath, but Fuzzy, wanting to be head-cook and bottle washer, also went for it at full speed. There was a violent collision of heads and both collapsed. The police put their first-aid skills to immediate use and Jack soon recovered, but not only was Fuzzy still unconscious, he was also bleeding profusely from a cut on his forehead. A car was procured and both went off to the Infirmary. Fuzzy regained consciousness, his wound received several stitches and he was kept in hospital over the weekend. Needless to say the match was abandoned — just as well for the police in view of their awful start.

Fuzzy came back to school after about a week and throughout May he kept us up to date on Wally Hammond's progress towards the record of scoring 1,000 runs by the end of the month. His enthusiasm for cricket was quite infectious — Latin was a poor second at this time. The feat had only been recorded twice previously, the last time by Tom Hayward way back in 1900, so our excitement can be well imagined. At last, with only one day to go to the end of the month, Hammond made it and included in his total were five centuries. After this, it was back to Latin with a vengeance, homework had to be up to scratch — or else, for Fuzzy reverted to the disciplinarian who would stand no nonsense.

June 29th, 1927 was a never-to-be forgotten day, both locally and nationally. It was not only the 700th Anniversary of the Granting of a Charter to Salisbury by Henry III in 1227 but also a once-in-a-lifetime occasion, for we had a total eclipse of the sun. For weeks, "Billy" Brewer, our physics master, fed us information on the forthcoming — quite unique — event: how privileged we would be to witness the eclipse, how there had not been one visible in Great Britain for the five hundred-odd years between 1140 and 1715, how the next one would not occur until the year 2151, how there would be an almost total eclipse in the year 1999, how by that time he would be long dead, how a few of us might live to see it but even so we would be very old men. In fact he almost frightened us to death — it was as though he was discussing the end of the world.

We were all up early on the great day and then, sure enough, at about six o'clock the sky began to darken. Dusk was somewhat early that morning — it was an uncanny atmosphere. It got darker and darker. Then, at about six thirty, there was complete darkness for almost half a minute. All the time we were watching through smoked glass — prepared by holding a piece of clear glass over a lighted candle. The period of total darkness seemed never ending. Then, slowly there appeared a small rim of light. In another half hour it was all over for another two hundred-odd years and we began to prepare for the celebration of seven hundred years since Salisbury became a city.

The day had been declared a public holiday and all shops and businesses were closed. Unfortunately, whether as a result of the eclipse or for some other reason, both that day and the next two were ruined by rain that was torrential at times. This was most unfortunate for preparations to ensure a truly memorable occasion had been in hand for over a year.

Just before ten o'clock, with my father, mother and young sister (she was not yet four), I went to Blue Boar Row to watch the arrival of the official guests at the Council House (now the Guildhall). Precisely at 10.40am, led by the Chief Constable, Mr Frank Richardson, a truly stately procession left via Blue Boar Row, Minster Street, Silver Street and High Street to make its way to the Cathedral for a service at 11 o'clock.

Behind the Chief Constable was a party of the city police followed by Mr Telford bearing the mace. He was a splendid figure and was, I believe, a former police sergeant. Then came the Mayor, Councillor Hudson (managing director of the Salisbury Times), accompanied by the High Sheriff, the General Officer Commanding Southern Command and a high-ranking officer of the Royal Air Force. Next was Mr Hugh Morrison, the Member of Parliament, and the Recorder and various representatives from the courts. Following them were no less than twelve mayors from Wiltshire, Hampshire and Dorset. Each was accompanied by their respective mace bearer and town clerk. I have a vivid memory of one extremely tall and well built bearer, who stood out like a sore thumb. Instead of the truly magnificent maces borne by his colleagues, he was marching, very pompously, carrying a small lidded chalice about nine inches high. I believe he represented one of the North West Wiltshire towns.

Then came the other two city mace bearers followed by the aldermen and councillors, the Town Clerk, the City Surveyor, the City Accountant, magistrates, representatives of city organisations and finally another squad of police. It was possibly the most splendid and at the same time dignified procession in the city's history. During the service in the Cathedral, the sermon was preached by the Bishop and the final hymn was one which had been specially written for the occasion by the Dean and set to music by the organist, Doctor W. Alcock MVO, who had been a music tutor to the Royal family.

For many years the council offices had been in Endless Street, next to the Palace Theatre, in accommodation that became more and more cramped by the year. In 1926, Dr Bourne, who had lived for many years at St Edmund's College in Bedwin Street, had died and the city fathers purchased the house and extensive grounds. The house was renovated to become the new civic offices, while the grounds provided the public with a beautiful ready made park. This purchase coincided with the Seven Hundredth Anniversary Year and so immediately after the completion of the Cathedral service, the procession reformed and went to the old St Edmund's College, which was then dedicated to become the new Council House. The procession returned via the Market Place to the old Council House which was then renamed the Guildhall.

After all this strenuous activity, no doubt the civic dignitaries, none of whom were in the first flush of youth, required refreshment. This was immediately forthcoming as they sat down to a splendid banquet.

They had little time for dalliance as a truly magnificent procession had been arranged to start at three o'clock from the Close. From here it made its way via High Street, Crane Street, Harcourt Terrace, Dews Road, Fisherton Street, The Canal, Queen Street, Blue Boar Row and Castle Street to Victoria Park. There were four bands and all branches of Salisbury's many organisations and athletic clubs were represented. I have a lasting memory of the Swimming Club, attired very correctly in view of the heavy rain in bedraggled swimming costumes (suits came later), and each and every member looking as though they had great difficulty in stopping their teeth from chattering.

Without doubt the star attraction was the procession within a procession that brought up the rear — Seven Hundred Years of Salisbury. No expense had been spared — the popular Mr Frank Stevens, Curator of the Salisbury and Blackmore Museum, had written the history and this had been licked into shape by Mrs Herbert Richardson, who most certainly must have had a great feeling for the subject. There were seven sections (each representing a hundred years), each headed by two Scouts who held aloft a scroll giving the date, eg 1227-1327, beautifully executed in Trajan Roman lettering by the School of Art.

As the procession passed so the history of Salisbury came to life. For me it was a milestone — suddenly I became aware of my good fortune in being a native of the city. It was the start of a love affair that has lasted well over sixty years and I have spent many happy hours in studying the city's past.

In the first section, 1227-1327, we saw King Henry III, preceded by his clerk, bearing the new Royal Charter. The king was followed by Hubert de Burgh, Bishop Richard Poore, founder of the new Cathedral and city, the first mayor of New Sarum, and William Longuespee, son of Henry II, Earl of Salisbury and Sheriff of Wiltshire. Then came Bishop Bingham who built Ayleswade Bridge at Harnham, which brought prosperity to the new city, and next several friars with their warden, representing the Francescan convent built on land which is now the Friary. All the characters except the friars were dressed in beautifully rich garments and despite the rain produced a truly magnificent spectacle.

Featured in the section representing the period 1327-1427 was King Edward III, who spent a great deal of his time when not fighting battles at his great palace at Clarendon, four miles from the city. He rode in the procession flanked by his two prisoners — King David of Scotland and John of France. Next came two local benefactors — John Chandeler and Dame Agnes Bottenham, who together founded the Trinity Hospital.

The next century saw the peak of the English wool trade and the two bitter enemies of that period, John Halle, who was mayor no less than four times, and William Swayne, mayor on three occasions, who walked side by side arguing away. Both left their marks — for we still have the Halle of John Halle and Swayne is remembered by Swaynes Close and Swayne's Chapel in St Thomas' Church. The two were very different characters — Swayne the upright business man, Halle, somewhat violent, perhaps the wideboy of his time, who was sent to prison for using obscene language towards the king.

The two traders were followed by the infamous Richard III. Next came a headsman, carrying a mighty axe which was pointing to the poor Duke of Buckingham, walking closely behind with hands tied together. The duke, beheaded in the Market Place, is reputed to haunt the building which formerly housed Style and Gerrish (now

The British Legion's entries in the 700th Anniversary celebrations passing Lloyds Bank on Blue Boar Row. Horses were still popular for local deliveries in 1927.

St Christopher, the Tailors' Guild giant, made one of his infrequent excursions from the Museum as a leading light in the 700th Anniversary celebrations. It is doubtful if he had ever seen a wetter day in his four-hundred-odd-year life.

Debenhams). During the nineteenth century, a headless skeleton was discovered when alterations were being made. The Blue Boar Inn formerly stood on this site.

The period 1527-1627 was led by a pageant representing a procession such as the City Guilds had in Tudor times. Once again the tailors' giant, St Christopher, attended by his Hob-Nob, made an appearance. They were accompanied by country boys and girls dancing to the music of a flute. Behind them came Thomas Brickett (remembered by Bricketts Hospital in Exeter Street). He was accompanied by Christopher Weekes, who laid the foundation stone of the timbered Council House, which stood on the war memorial site. This was destroyed by fire in 1780 and the present Guildhall then built. One of Salisbury's great literary figures, Philip Massenger, poet, dramatist and contemporary of William Shakespeare, walked with Henry Lawes, a native of Dinton and musician to the court of Charles I. Finally came King James I who gave the city its Charter of Incorporation — this constituted the governing body as "the Mayor and Commonalty of the City of New Sarum".

Heading the next section, representing 1627-1727, was John Ivie, mayor of the city, who stayed at his post during a terrible visitation of the plague. Deserted by his colleagues, who fled, he, with his Sergeant at Mace and his serving man and maid, managed to keep order in the city against the pestilence, famine and riot. He is still remembered today, for we have Ivy Street — what a shame that the spelling of his name should have been corrupted.

The Civil War was portrayed by two characters, Colonel Ludlow, a Cromwellian, and Sir Marmaduke Langdale, a Royalist leader. Under Ludlow, the Parliamentarians held the city in 1645, stabled their horses in the cathedral and fortified the Old Belfry. The Royalists under Langdale then forced their enemies to retreat after a famous skirmish around the Poultry Cross and Market Place. I remember that as a very small boy, my mother pointed out to me scars on the great west doors of the Cathedral and said they had been caused by bullets fired by Cromwellians. She might have been correct for her family was possibly living in the city during the Civil War and the story was probably passed down from generation to generation.

Then followed two tragic gentlemen, Colonel John Penruddocke of Compton Chamberlayne Park and Major Hugh Grove, who led an unsuccessful rebellion against Cromwell in 1655. At first it seemed successful. They and their followers rode into the city and captured both the Judge and the Sheriff. But they then met with failure and both were beheaded at Exeter.

A gentleman followed, and it was thanks to his generosity that I became, in 1930, an indentured apprentice. John, Duke of Somerset, in 1674 bequeathed £3,000 for "the apprenticing of poor children, born within the City of New Sarum". Behind him, preceded by sober-sided Puritans, came richly dressed Cavaliers of Charles II's reign.

The next period, 1727-1827, was entitled A Century of Humanity. It saw the foundation of the Infirmary — the first to be established in Wiltshire. Lord Feversham, Member of Parliament for Old Sarum — "the rottenest borough of them all", later MP for Downton, whose bequest of £500 in 1763 enabled the building of the Infirmary to commence in 1766, walked with the Duke of Queensberry, who laid the foundation stone. Both were remembered, by Feversham and Queensberry Wards. Behind these two benefactors walked William, first Earl of Radnor, the Infirmary's first president, and Henry, tenth Earl of Pembroke, the first visitor.

The pageant of this century was brought to a conclusion by George III, a frequent visitor to the city with his family as they made their way to Weymouth, which the King loved. Under the nom-de-plume of A gentleman of Berkshire he presented the Cathedral with a new and extremely fine organ. The instrument is now, I believe, still in use at St Thomas' Church.

The final section of the pageant, covering 1827-1927, in reality did not go beyond 1840, as it was thought the period following that time was within living memory. It was led by a carriage in which rode the Duchess of Kent, with her daughter, Princess (later Queen) Victoria, who visited the city in 1830 and stayed with Mr Wadham Wyndham at St Edmund's College.

Following on foot was Mr William Bird Brodie, first Member of Parliament after the Reform Bill of 1832, banker, owner of the Salisbury and Winchester Journal and Colonel of the Salisbury Corps of Volunteers. He was the gentleman who paid my great grandfather to take his place in the Troop of Yeomanry, which set out to fight in the Peninsular War in Spain in 1808. His bank later failed and he left the city a ruined man.

Finally the pageant was completed by four of the new 1840 City Police bringing up the rear. Called Peelers after their founder, Sir Robert Peel (hence we call police Bobbies), they brought law and order to the city after the riots of the 1830s.

As the end of the procession passed, spectators fell in behind and thousands thronged towards Victoria Park, where plenty of free entertainment had been arranged — athletics, tug-of-war, boxing, a tennis tournament, miniature golf championship, open-air concert and music by several bands. Despite the awful weather the people of Salisbury made the most of a well organised day.

We, as a family, made our way for tea to number 40, Waters Road, one of the recently erected council houses. Dad's workmate Mr Tom Bussell had moved there with his family from their Laverstock home in 1926. The new estate was being built on the old Fairfield, where a few years earlier, I had played football in the Cubs' League. Waters was the first road to be built and was named after a former mayor who had been an auctioneer and valuer, and was well respected, especially by the farming community.

After tea it was a question of waiting for night to fall, as this never-to-be-forgotten day ended on a high note with a fancy dress parade and torchlight procession back to the Market Place. Rockets were fired, blue and gold fires (the city's colours) were lit at Old Sarum and for the first time in my life, I saw the Cathedral illuminated. It was a glorious sight. I am sure we all went to bed that night worn out by some twelve hours of continuous festivities.

When we awoke the next day, which had been earmarked as the children's celebration, it was raining even more heavily. The great procession of more than 3,000 children was due to start from Exeter Street at three o'clock. At half past two, dressed in cricket shirt and white flannels (my very first pair of long-uns), with school cap on my head, I made my way to Bishop's school playground in almost torrential rain. Few of my colleagues arrived — at three o'clock it was decided to wait until four so we sheltered in school. I remember that it seemed very cold. At four o'clock it was decided to wait until five, at five we had to wait until six and at six the procession was postponed until the following day, July 1st.

The Friday which dawned was almost worse than the previous day. My mother had done a grand job on my flannels, which had been washed after my return home, somewhat bedraggled, on the Thursday evening, and there I was already dressed and back to school at 2.30pm. The same decisions were taken: wait until four o'clock, wait until five o'clock, wait until six o'clock, and then, glory be, it stopped raining.

We were now given little time and started to line up in the playground. Outside, in Exeter Street, a squad of police arrived to head the procession. They were followed by the Mayor and Mayoress in an open car and then hundreds of girls from five schools, who lined up in readiness to portray May Day revels as they progressed through the city streets.

The Band of the Royal Air Force from Old Sarum was stationed by the school gate and promptly at six o'clock the much delayed performance started. Our school was led by a mounted herald, followed by a pageant representing Salisbury children through the ages. Next came the girls of the school in white blouses and navy skirts. We followed in blue blazers with our white flannels. At least that was the idea, but at the rear came some thirty or so of us whose parents had not been able to afford the quite expensive blazers, so we were provided with cricket bats and tennis rackets to carry. This idea of "Tarzan" Taylor's had a rather humorous spin-off, because as we processed the public thought we were the school's outstanding cricketers and tennis stars. If the weather had been fine, I am sure the ranks of navy blue and white would have looked most impressive, but after more than forty eight hours of rain we were splashed with mud very, very quickly.

Our school was followed by Harnham with a representation of an old Friendly Society — the Besom Club. Then came St Osmund's with Midsummer Revels. The Choristers and Godolphin schools really went to town with splendid tableaux of their respective histories. They preceded my old school, St Martin's, which with girls from George Herbert's showed Christmas Revels through the Ages. I remember that they were led by several of my former schoolmates pulling on ropes that propelled a massive trolley on which was a yule-log some four feet in diameter, six feet in length, and most impressive. There was a secret to their apparent strength.

The log had been hollowed out by Mr Ralph Shergold, one of my former teachers. The two ends had been carefully sawn off and replaced. The final result looked most authentic.

The St Edmund's girls who followed had chosen a Mothering Sunday from the Middle Ages as their theme, while the boys from that school really enjoyed their tableau, which represented quarter-staff bouts in the days of Robin Hood.

Even the small private schools had entered into the spirit of things as there were tableaux by the Misses Milles School, the Clive School and the High School for Girls. The Modern School for Boys portrayed Modern Sports, while Leehurst Convent School did another representation of Children through the Seven Centuries.

St Mark's Boys' entry was rather fun. They portrayed the various side shows which might have been seen at Salisbury Fair during the Elizabethan period: barefisted boxing, wrestling, rope dancing, the quack doctor and Merry Andrew, whose job was to attract a crowd.

The Picture House, Fisherton Street, in 1928. Built as a Primitive Methodist Chapel in 1869, it became redundant in 1916 when the Dews Road Church was built. A cinema from then until 1937, it became in turn a Forces Recruiting Office, an Army depot, the Garrison Theatre, the Arts Theatre and finally the Playhouse.

The St Thomas' Boys' School tableau was in two parts. Firstly, there was Recruiting in 1756 for the King's Own Regiment of Foot, which was commanded by Lieutenant General Wolfe, of Quebec fame. This represented a true episode in the city's history when Salisbury lads were invited "to repair to Captain George Borrowdaile's in Brown Street to serve His Majesty King George". Their second tableau showed Backswood Contests, which had great popularity at fair times, when men would arrive from long distances to take part.

Highbury Avenue Boys became strolling players with a puppet show, of which people were very fond in the Middle Ages. The players were all in Tudor costume and a friend of mine who took part remembers how the dyes ran after the terrible soaking which the material experienced.

Finally came the Old Sarum Archers by St Paul's Boys' School and Street Vendors by Bemerton.

The mind boggles at the hours and hours which hundreds of parents and teachers must have put in to produce this wonderful display and ponders why the Good Lord could not have entered into the spirit of the occasion and given the event some decent weather.

Infants at school in the city were supposed to have a special entertainment and tea at the new Council House grounds on the Friday afternoon. I can't remember what happened to this event — was it postponed until Saturday? I don't know — my young sister who would have taken part has been in America for over forty years — I shall have to ask her one day.

There was quite an exciting innovation on the Friday and Saturday of that week. A film of the Wednesday's celebrations was shown at the Picture House. We thought it was amazing, though I expect today's youngsters would look on that silent black and white film as pretty poor entertainment. How times have changed.

In July, our Scout troop, 15th Salisbury (St Martin's) played a cricket match between showers — it really was a wet summer — against 1st Bemerton. Their Scoutmaster was the Rev Hayter, the curate, a gentleman rather noted for his idiosyncratic ways, who arranged for the game to be played on the Bemerton field in Lower Road. On arrival, we discovered the grass on the pitch was some four or five inches long. Bemerton won the toss and we started, but it was quite farcical because I found the only way to ensure the ball reached the wicket at the other end was to bowl yorkers. Unfortunately, one of my deliveries hit a batsman on the forehead and off he had to go for stitching at the Infirmary. The game was then abandoned and the batsman, who came to Bishop Wordsworth's School the following term, never allowed me to forget the incident.

It went on raining almost throughout the summer holidays that followed, when two incidents stand out. The first was the opening of F.W. Woolworth in what had been for many, many years, David Stevens — General Draper, Milliner, Haberdasher, Hosier and Glover (as the massive fascia board had proclaimed). In those days Woolworth's was a very different business to the one we know today. Then it was a store with two prices, threepence and sixpence — nothing over a tanner. How we peered through the windows in the week prior to the official opening at nine o'clock on a Saturday morning. The great day arrived and with two friends I queued — we were possibly the first inside. There were many bargains, no doubt the store wanted to make a good impression. Ladies were seemingly attracted by a special display of enamel saucepans. These were in three sizes at a price of sixpence for the saucepan and sixpence for the lid. This was the way that Woolworth's got round their well known slogan of "nothing over sixpence". I ran home and told my mother, who quickly dispatched me with a shilling to buy one of those really cheap saucepans. When I got back she was so pleased with the undoubted bargain that I was again dispatched to buy two more. There was a snag because a sign read: "only one saucepan to each customer". On the way I met an old school friend, who very kindly came with me and in no time we had each purchased a saucepan and lid. I presume that they were what are known today as "loss-leaders" for they represented excellent value and my mother had them in daily use over many years. I remember that my friend and I carried the saucepans well away from "Woollies" before he handed the one he had bought on my behalf over to me, just in case we had broken the law and might be prosecuted.

The following week, I heard that my school friend (we had been at St Martin's Infants' and Boys' School together, prior to moving on to Bishop Wordsworth's) George Fulford had broken his right leg and was in the Infirmary. I went several times to visit him and discovered what had happened. He had been tree climbing in the Friary Recreation Ground (this has long since vanished) and in trying to show off in front of a girl, had a nasty fall. The young lady concerned had been in our class at the infants' school, and in a photo of 1921 there is George standing next to her (was it a case of love at first sight?). He was in hospital for several weeks and after discharge had his leg in plaster and started back at school after the holidays on crutches. I saw him some ten years ago, just before his death, and apparently he was still troubled by the result of that accident *cherchez la femme.*

When we arrived back after the holidays, we found that school was somewhat altered as the girls had departed to the South Wilts Grammar School for Girls, recently erected in Stratford Road. The mistresses had also vamoosed so we had masters only. Two newcomers had arrived: "Tich" Oram, who taught history and was an excellent soccer player, and a six-footer, "Bags" Robertson, so called because of the very wide flannels or Oxford Bags which he always wore — they were probably at least twenty six inches round the bottoms. He taught both English and French and I remember he had an extremely pretty wife.

The departure of the girls meant that the playground which they had used was now empty, but the iron gates which led to it were secured by a massive padlock. Around the perimeter of the playground were some extremely fine apple trees laden with beautiful, ripening fruit. About a week after our return for the Autumn Term, one lunchtime I had to dash to Miss Tylee's for my mother to get some cotton and it was indeed fortunate that this errand almost made me late for afternoon school, as it saved me from a caning. I just made lines before the bell stopped tolling and off we went across the road to Bishopgate and started our lesson. This was interrupted by the arrival of the headmaster, Mr Reuben Bracher, a very powerful man, who burst into the room carrying a cane. He looked really angry.

"Stand up, all those who have been the girls' playground this lunchtime." There were only about two others beside myself who did not get immediately to their feet. One by one the rest had to go to the front of the class to be caned — and I mean CANED, one on each hand by the Old Man. When he had finished he went through the back of our room into the Lower Sixth and we heard the caning repeated all over again. I don't think I've ever seen a man more angry. After school, I learned what it was all about — someone had produced a hacksaw, sawn through the massive padlock which secured the gates and almost the whole school had gone into the girls' playground and stripped the apple trees. No wonder the Old Man was cross, he probably had his eye on the fruit for himself and friends. That day, even though he was due to retire in the following July, he caned about three hundred boys — six hundred cuts in total. His anger possibly lent him strength.

During the half-term holiday in early November, I went down with chicken pox, caught from my young sister. She was four and so suffered only a mild attack. I was thirteen and nearly lost my life, being covered with the tell-tale pustules — they were everywhere. As my mother said later on many occasions: "You couldn't put a sixpence between them." The holiday was for two days, a Monday and Tuesday. I began to feel under the weather on Monday evening. By Tuesday evening the spots had appeared and Dr "Willie" Gordon came to see me next morning. The following day I was a great deal worse — the pustules had become scabs and a message was sent to the doctor, who came mid-morning, afternoon and again in late evening. I have never forgotten that day — my condition can be deduced from the fact that a fire was lit in the bedroom, something which never happened unless there was serious illness. In my more lucid moments I thought that perhaps I was going to die — the room seemed to come and go, one moment in focus, the next seen through a worsening mist.

That evening, the whole family, with the exception of my eldest sister who was still at Bristol University, sat around my bed talking in whispers. Their faces and whispered conversation came and went. Finally I fell into a deep sleep and awoke next morning in a bed that had become wet with sweat to find that I felt so much better I was almost back to normal. I think it was a close run thing, but as a result the doctor said: "No more school until January." This meant that owing to a variety of childhood illnesses I lost almost half a school year during 1927.

Chapter Two 1928
Into my teens

The year 1928 was a far better time for me healthwise, and as a result I was able to really get stuck into my school work. During that year, in contrast to the previous one, I was not absent for a single day.

Early in January, I had to start classes in preparation for confirmation. Both my name and that of my friend, Harry Akroyd, had been left off the list for a class that had started several weeks earlier and as a result of this mix-up we had to go to a special class for just the two of us, taken by the Reverend W.N. Willson, at St Martin's Rectory.

The Confirmation Service was to be held on Sunday, March 25th. A week or so before that date, the Rector said that the following week he would like to see us separately. Harry went on Friday evening and reported back to me before my appointment on the Saturday afternoon. Apparently we had to be acquainted with "the facts of life". I don't know who was most embarrassed — the Rector or me. He produced two little books, handed me one, and together we read all about the birds and the bees. At this time I was thirteen, Harry was a year older and the books were written in language suitable for eight-year-olds, dating possibly from the height of Victorian prudery. I remember the opening sentence "You have probably noticed between your legs there is an organ through which you pass water". This, at thirteen, I ask you! At last the ordeal ended and I made my escape to immediately join Harry. We compared notes and spent the rest of the afternoon convulsed in laughter at the antics of adults. No doubt the knowledge we had both gained in the school playground had many gaps but was far more advanced than that given us by the Rector.

The great day arrived, I remember it was wet. Harry and I, as members of the 15th Salisbury St Martin's Scout Troop, wore our uniforms. He was second in the Bear Patrol, I had the same rank in the Hawks. We marched up smartly together, to be confirmed by a bishop from Africa. Then, as we had been the second pair, we sat and waited while he laid hands on some sixty others.

A fortnight later, we both made our first communion — a somewhat nerve-racking occasion. Dad seldom accompanied my mother and sisters, who always went on the first Sunday of each month, but this time he could not escape. Mum said it was his duty to take his only son to first communion, so he accompanied Harry and I to the six o'clock service, thus avoiding the crowd which always filled the church at seven and eight o'clock each Easter.

Harry came with us because his father had been killed during the war and as his mother had to work in London, he lived with his grandmother in Paynes Hill. We had an extremely happy relationship — he was more daring than me but I was rather better at sports. Later that year, in November, he came to tell me that he was leaving school the following week and going to London to live with his mother and stepfather, as she had remarried. I only ever saw him again for about ten minutes in 1932, when he came to Salisbury to visit his grandmother. By then he was the proud possessor of an old motorbike, on which he had ridden from London. Unfortunately, the day of his visit coincided with my sister's wedding, so that our renewal of acquaintance was cut drastically short. On the outbreak of war, Harry, who had already qualified as a pilot, joined the Royal Air Force. During the Battle of Britain he flew a Spitfire in 152 Squadron based at Warmwell, near Weymouth. On the afternoon of Monday, October 7th, 1940 the squadron engaged the enemy (whose target was Yeovil) over Lyme Bay. Harry was shot down and the plane crashed and burned out at Shillingstone, near Blandford. He died from severe burns the next day and is buried in the tiny churchyard of Holy Trinity, Warmwell. I always called Harry "Aky" and his nickname for me was "Maido". It's quite uncanny that the call sign of his Spitfire Squadron was "Maida".

To go back to 1928. On Easter Monday, all the troops in the Salisbury and District Scout Association caught the train to Tisbury. This was in connection with the Grose Trophy which was held at a different venue each year. On this occasion, when we reached Tisbury, we marched against a biting wind to the top of Chilmark Down, a distance of almost four miles. We arrived there in mid-morning to be greeted by heavy rain that very quickly turned to sleet, then hail. After shivering for about an hour, doing nothing but wait for an improvement in the weather, it was decided that the rain was in for the day and we started the long trek back to the station, where we waited a considerable time for a train and even then some poor unfortunates had to be left to catch the next one. It was no-one's fault but were we cold!

A month or so after Easter, my mother informed me on a Saturday evening that she and Harry's grandmother had agreed with a church worker from St Martin's that we could carry the candles during the Sunday evening services. Neither of us were very keen, but in those days you didn't argue with your elders so on the Sunday evening there we were in the vestry, arrayed in red cassocks and white surplices which were trimmed with lace. We felt a couple of right Charleys and when we processed it seemed that every eye was on us. Of course we had a great deal of banter from our friends but continued to do the job and suffer in silence. The church worker, a middle-aged bachelor, seemed well disposed towards us and we were invited to his house for supper after services. However, a few weeks later he revealed his true colours when he tried an unsuccessful pass at us. We made our escape and after that gave him a wide berth, although we never mentioned a word to a soul. In retrospect we ought to have reported him immediately, as to my knowledge he was still chasing choirboys twenty-odd years later and I don't suppose we were the first to be propositioned.

Between Easter and Whitsun that year, a task set us by "Tich" Oram, the history master, was to have a great effect on the rest of my life. We were asked to produce charts showing the development of castles. I found that this was right up my street, went to it with gusto and soon finished the illustrations. I was rather stumped by the required lettering until the intervention of my eldest sister, who was on holiday from university. She suggested that I borrowed her lettering pens and I discovered that I really enjoyed using them. My chart was placed first in the class, as was the next one

which dealt with churches. From that time, I began to study
lettering and decided that this was what I wanted to do after
leaving school. Strange really, because my mother's father, a
skilled painter and decorator, could also produce the occasional
sign. I think that I have much to thank Mr Oram for — it is
amazing how a small happening can change the direction of one's
life.

On a glorious Sunday afternoon, a week or so after Whitsun,
Acky and I were wandering along after Bible Class when we met
two girls who had been confirmed at the same time as us. Whether
it was the sunshine or that we had reached the age for puppy love I
don't know, but I can still see them now, looking most attractive in
their white confirmation dresses. Harry was the first to speak to
them — being almost a year older he usually took the lead. We
strolled along together, Acky in front with P--- R---, who had two
extremely long ginger (sorry auburn) plaits. I brought up the rear
with her friend V--- R---, she was quite pretty with short dark hair,
cut in the fashionable shingle of the late twenties. This was the
first time that I had really noticed either of them.

We went through into the Cathedral Close and sat on the grass
on the north side, near the stone stile leading to Bishop's Walk.
There we stayed chatting and laughing for what seemed ages. Our
laughter attracted the attention of the Close Constable, a retired
policeman, who walked slowly towards us and, in very stern
language, ordered us to leave the Close. "Didn't we realise that it
was Sunday". How different from the present day when the Close
lawns are filled with people of all ages, squatting on the grass. Off
we went, rather shamefaced, said goodbye to the girls and arranged
to meet the following Sunday. On the next Wednesday, Mum said
"Who were the two girls that you and Harry were in the Close with
on Sunday?" We had been observed by one of her close friends —
it was amazing how one or other of them always seemed to be
reporting my actions back to her. Nothing escaped Mum, I expect
the episode was relayed to Dad, but he never mentioned it. We saw
the girls quite often and chatted — they told their friends that we
were their boys and no doubt heard the sound of wedding bells, but
within a couple of months, I was pleased when V--- told me that she
was going out with another friend of mine. Now I could resume the

really important things in life, like cricket, Scouts and also the new attraction, boating on the river.

I don't know how we first got hooked on this. True, Mum and Dad had often talked of how they used to enjoy it, of how on one occasion Dad lost an oar and had to pay quite a bit in compensation. Anyhow, one Sunday afternoon we managed to find one shilling and sixpence and with this money went off to Castle Street and hired a four-oared boat. There were two boat houses, the one on the Castle Street side was run by an old couple named Sheppard — they were a lovely pair, ready to put up with four youngsters making their first essay in the art of rowing. They were always pleased to see you and although the boats were quite old, we patronised them in preference to the opposition, Elliott's on the far bank.

Their boats were very different, much newer and always beautifully varnished, but Mr Elliott gave the impression that he was doing his customers a favour. He could have used a little of the

Boating on the river — a pleasant and peaceful pastime (when flies were absent) enjoyed by generations of Salisbury citizens.

Sheppards' charm. We always tossed for the right to have first row — there was little art about it, the boat would cross from bank to bank, often bringing remonstrations from the more experienced, who never seemed to have any bother in keeping a straight course. Long before we reached the sharp, right-angled bend in the river at Black Well, the two non-rowers would be clamouring for their turn. We would change positions, one at a time, but even so, the boat would rock alarmingly. Onlookers on the bank waited for one or other of us to fall into the fast flowing Avon, which at Black Well has quite treacherous currents. Fortunately no accidents occurred, the Lord looked after us, rightly so for we had just been to Bible Class.

Boating became a Sunday afternoon outing. Our rowing improved rapidly, soon we were able to feather the oars and shortly after that we tried double canoes, they were great fun — much better than mooning about with soppy girls. When the Bible Class outing to Weymouth came along, immediately on arrival we made a beeline for the beach to hire a boat for four. The owner insulted us by asking if we could row — what a question! By this time we looked upon ourselves as experts. We took off, and when about half a mile from shore tried our changing oarsmen technique, to discover the sea was very different from the placid Avon. The boat tipped to such a degree that we were shipping water. We gave up the manoeuvre, which had not gone unnoticed from the beach. On our return the owner used expletives which I, for one, had never heard before — he even cast doubts on our ancestry. After that, we stuck to the Avon and the safety of Sheppards' boats.

With two other friends, Harry Akroyd and I formed the Trinity Cycling Club. The name was borrowed from Trinity Street where Tom Dennis, one of the friends, lived. We solemnly drew up a set of rules, signed membership forms and then had some truly memorable rides to Southampton, Bournemouth and Christchurch, during which time I can't remember one of us suffering a puncture or any sort of a breakdown.

During the summer, a collection was taken at school so that a presentation could be made to the "Old Man", Mr Reuben Bracher, who was retiring after thirty eight years as headmaster. I remember that when this was done, Vincent, the head boy, gave a rambling and much too long speech, during which he ran his finger around his collar every few seconds. Although most of us laughed about this later, few would have wanted to exchange positions with him.

My summer holiday during 1928 was one of the happiest I had experienced. The first two weeks I mooched around, bored to tears. Then one dinner time Dad came home and asked if I would like to go and help him at work that afternoon. He was still employed at Farr's, the Brown Street coach-builders, and the boy who had done the odd jobs had recently left. Dad had asked Mr Frank Farr if I could help out during the holidays. I did all sorts of jobs — turning the handle that worked the bellows of the fire in the smithy, taking complete springs from cars in readiness for resetting, running errands for all and sundry, and cleaning the oil and grease from car parts with a wire brush and a bucket of paraffin. In short, I thoroughly enjoyed work and got quite dirty in the process. At the end of each week Mr Farr presented me with half-a-crown, so I became rich compared with my usual pocket money of sixpence.

I remember how on a Monday, in the middle of my spell of work, Dad and I went home to dinner to find the rest of the family in a state of excitement. At about ten o'clock that morning, sparks from a passing train had set fire to the thatched roofs of a row of cottages at Petersfinger, many people had rushed to the scene and had witnessed a fierce conflagration. All five cottages were destroyed in less than two hours. Mum and two of my sisters had gone and they gave Dad and I graphic descriptions, which left me feeling somewhat cheated by having missed the free show.

On September 22nd, I reached the age of fourteen and the insurance policy which my mother had taken on my life ten years before matured, so I was presented with a brand new racing bike which had dropped handlebars. Dad insisted, however, that the handlebars were too low for a boy so another pair were fixed which rather spoilt the sporty look. The cycle was purchased at Halfords and had been reduced in price from five pounds ten shillings to four pounds ten shillings. I had five years of real pleasure from that bike — Dad disposed of my old bitza to a friend for the princely sum of one pound.

One afternoon, during a break at the end of the summer term, we had caught sight of the newly appointed head, who was with Mr Bracher. The new man, only thirty eight years of age, was Captain F.C. Happold DSO, who had taught at a school in Cambridge. He too stayed at Bishop Wordsworth's until retirement and made many changes, not all of which in his early days met with the approval of the governors. Some of his new ideas were put into being on the first day of the autumn term. The school was divided into six houses, all named after bishops, I was in Berkeley, the others being Dunstan, Becket, Wolsey, Trelawny and Ridley. Each had a housemaster and two assistant housemasters. A house meeting was held each month and from these we learned how formal meetings should be conducted, as minutes were taken, which were read and confirmed at the following meeting. We had leagues for soccer and cricket, both at junior and senior level. Athletics became a feature and cross-country runs were introduced during the winter months.

Each house had a different colour and I well remember the day that I went home with my newly acquired soccer jersey in the Berkeley colour of yellow, tried it on, and was christened by Dad "the yellow peril". For a few weeks, we had to try a new system — instead of masters coming to our classroom, they stayed put and we had to go to them — this was one of "Happy's" ideas of the genus Dud, but at least he soon saw the chaos that his new scheme was producing. A great deal of time was wasted between lessons as some three hundred and fifty boys made their way from one class to another.

The new head rather upset parents when in October, only some six weeks after the start of term, he decreed that our headgear should be redesigned. Until now our navy blue caps had just carried the school coat of arms, three bells on a shield and a bishop's crook. Now, in addition, caps had to have two bands of light blue. As this was only a try-out, the school outfitters had bands of pale blue braid stitched on to existing stock. We were only given a month before everyone was expected to wear the new design. This meant three hundred and fifty-odd perfectly good caps were consigned to the rubbish bin — and they cost three shillings and ninepence each! Happy further enraged parents when he changed the caps again at the commencement of the summer term of that school year, now they had one pale blue band only. These were of a permanent nature (and more expensive) for the band was now of a material set into the dark blue surround. Each and every boy, even the upper sixth had to wear a cap, although usually as soon as we were out of sight of school they were folded up and carried in a pocket. We all took this chance, but if seen by a master it brought at least a severe "impot", or imposition, of perhaps two hundred lines — "I must wear my school cap at all times". Impots were a menace, they seemed to be handed out for the slightest misdemeanours. On one occasion I tried to shorten the job by fixing five pens together thus writing five lines at once, but soon realised that this was a waste of time.

In November of that year, I arrived home after school on a Tuesday afternoon to be greeted by a very excited mother who had just heard that King Amanullah of Afghanistan with his Queen Suriya would be leaving by train from Salisbury Southern Railway Station at about five o'clock. With Mum and my younger sister, Margaret, I dashed to find a tremendous crowd in South Western Road. The huge gate, some twenty-five feet wide, barred the public from the station yard, but we were able to see the King and Queen, who had been to Salisbury Plain to inspect new weapons. While in this country both had admired Western ways. The Queen ceased wearing the veil and had her hair cut short in the latest fashion, and they returned home determined to bring their country up to date. The people did not agree and revolted. As a result the King quickly restored the veil for women, but this did not satisfy the masses and he was deposed on January 14th, 1929.

One lunchtime, as we were all meandering along Catherine Street on our way home from school, we heard that a big fire had occurred in The Canal that morning. It is amazing just how quickly news of a disaster can spread and we dashed, with most of our school colleagues, to the scene. The blaze was at Madame Alice Harrison's — a rather à-la gown shop — and despite it happening during daylight hours, only the blackened shell of the three-storey building remained. Fortunately, all the staff managed to escape and the volunteer Fire Brigade prevented the flames spreading to adjoining buildings. For a few minutes we gazed at the still smoking ruins, then quickly made our way home, realising that "I went to see the fire" would hardly be accepted as an excuse for lateness at afternoon school.

Another memory from 1928 is the very gruesome story told us by a colleague after a Monday evening Scout parade. During that weekend, a man had taken his own life by lying on the Salisbury to Southampton railway line, near the Laverstock Road bridge. The driver of a train, on arriving in Salisbury, reported that he thought the engine had hit something — it had, the poor chap had been cut to pieces. L-- P--, one of our Patrol Leaders, he would have been about fifteen, a year or so older than me, was apprenticed to an undertaker and gave a vivid description of the recovery of the body and how a shovel was used to pick up the pieces. L--- was at that time a big, strong chap and told the story quite nonchalantly, as though it was all in a day's work. Unfortunately shortly afterwards he caught rheumatic fever, which left him a shadow of his former self, and he was never again well during the rest of his comparatively short life.

Chapter Three 1929
The ancestor of the Spit wins its spurs

Early in the New Year, I remember that just after the start of afternoon school it began snowing very heavily. After about half an hour, the order arrived via special messengers from the headmaster that all country boys were to go home immediately. The rest of us carried on, but when we left school at 4.15pm we found that the snow was some two feet deep and the drifting against the Close wall was up to five feet.

It was Scout Parade night and we had a wonderful time with a marvellous snow-fight. The following day, we were, of course, minus all our country colleagues and also a number of masters. Three forms were taught as one. As for our absentees, they were missing for a fortnight until a thaw set in. On their return, we heard harrowing tales of the journey which they had faced as they made their way home on that Monday afternoon. Their stories were not all exaggeration, however, for it was on record that one drift at Chilmark had been fifteen feet high.

That winter we had many days of frost and as a result enjoyed a great deal of sliding on the asphalt surface of the playground. These slides were made by watering an area some three feet in width — almost across the playground — before we left school in the evening. The following morning the treated section was like glass and we had a marvellous time at every opportunity: before school, at each break, and after school. Even two masters, "Fuzzy" Richards and "Tarzan" Taylor, left the safety of the Masters' Room to join in the fun, which was brought to an untimely end when a boy named Birch went on sliding. Just before colliding with the playground wall, he stuck his arm out to save himself and there was an awful crack as it was fractured. Slides were forbidden from then on and poor old Birch, instead of receiving sympathy, was looked upon as the chap who stopped all the fun.

We really felt the cold weather when we played the house soccer matches on Saturday mornings. The pavilion at the School Field was made of unlined corrugated iron and I have memories of changing in this building with both the trees around and the pitch white with frost. It was cold but I don't think we suffered any permanent harm — even though we had no showers or facilities of any kind.

The Saturday that I shall never forget occurred in March. In the morning my House, Berkeley, had a match against Ridley. I played at centre-forward, Jack Cope, a friend from Wilton, was the right-winger. We had a field day, for Jack scored four and I got a hat-trick in our 7-1 victory. Immediately after the game, I had to go home for a quick meal and with the rest of the St Martins' Scout team catch the bus to Fovant. Their pitch near the downs had quite a slope and, although we played with this in our favour, at half-time we were only drawing 2-2. In the second half we must have gone mad — despite playing up the hill — and we added five more. I myself banged in four of these and a very tired schoolboy got home in the seventh heaven of delight, having scored a total of seven goals (one for each heaven) during a day to be forever cherished.

Monday, April 1st, 1929 produced a well remembered occasion. To celebrate the festival of All Fools, each member of my class contributed one penny and with this money a "Tutankhamun's bat" was purchased from Wilton's Sports Shop on the corner of The Canal and Queen Street. It was a simple but clever device made of thin wire and paper and motivated by an elastic band, wound by means of a small propeller. When the band was absolutely tight the "bat" was placed into a small envelope, measuring about five inches by four inches, and sealed. The name Mr Warren was written on the front and the envelope placed on the master's desk just before the second lesson of the morning.

In came "Pimp", the deathly silence of anticipation broken by the usual "Good morning, Sir" chanted in unison. He said: "Good morning, Boys," as he somewhat absentmindedly opened the envelope. There was a sudden flutter and out flew the bat, which and exceeded our expectations by doing several circuits of the room. We shouted: "April Fool, Sir", and there were roars of laughter, which ceased very suddenly as he roared back: "QUIET". Again there was deadly silence and Pimp picked up the maths text book and said: "Turn to page so and so. As an extra homework during this week, you will each do the twenty problems set on that page." The lesson passed in a most subdued atmosphere.

The following morning, Pimp came into our room between lessons and said that he was sorry that he had lost his temper on the previous day and that he felt the imposition was much too harsh. (We thought he was going to let us off.) We were not to know that he had been suffering from toothache, so he had decided we need only do ten of the problems which he had set. In retrospect I think the real reason for his outburst was something to do with the fact that around this time he must have been informed that he was to lose his post, as he unfortunately did not possess a degree. This new rule was most unfair as Pimp was an excellent master. A month or so later he was appointed Head of Sherston in North Wilts and we were all sorry to see him go.

One of the new features introduced at school that year had been the introduction of history lectures given by each member of the class in turn. We were allowed to choose our subject from a long list — the talk had to last roughly twenty minutes. As I chose to talk on Salisbury Cathedral, finding enough subject matter was no problem, but I remember how the fatal day crept ever closer. This was the first time that I had spoken before an audience and though I spent a lot of time in preparation, including producing a quite large plan, gosh! I was scared. The morning arrived. The first lesson went all too quickly and before I had time to collect myself, "Tich" Oram had arrived and said: "I think Maidment is going to tell us all about the Cathedral this morning," as he retired to sit at the back of the class.

I gathered my notes and plan together, went out to the front as a lamb to the slaughter and nonchalantly pinned the drawing to the blackboard. I hoped no-one would notice my shaking hand as I performed the task which seemed to be taking an eternity. At last the job was done and I turned, faced the class and started to lecture. The first couple of minutes were truly terrifying but after that it was quite easy. It seemed no time at all before I got to the end of my talk — actually I had quite enjoyed the last quarter of an hour. With "Tich" Oram sitting at the back, the class had listened in silence. Now it was time for questions and then criticism from both the class and the master, who gave marks for research, presentation and delivery. This was on the morning prior to the Whitsun break and how I enjoyed that holiday — it was as if a great weight had been lifted from me. It taught me a lesson: if you are scared of something, just get on and tackle it, you will find that the reality is never half as bad as your imagination made it.

On that Friday afternoon before Whitsun, during the first lesson we were told to assemble in chapel as soon as the bell went. This we did, and found that all the masters were present and sitting in the seats usually reserved for the choir. We waited silently wondering what the dickens was in store for us. As we heard the approach of "Happy", the Head, we all stood as, in his usual fashion, he made his way from the door at the back of the chapel, gown flapping, then stopped and turned at the Chancel steps. "Sit down," he said. We sat. He started: "This afternoon, I have a most painful duty, one which, when I was appointed Headmaster, I hoped that I would never have to perform, BLANK Senior, stand up." The individual concerned was sitting next to the window at the end of the row behind me. We all turned and gazed as he rose to his feet with a very sickly grin, which no doubt was forced by the way his stomach was behaving. The Head then continued: "For several weeks boys in Form — have been complaining of theft of their belongings. At lunchtime today H—— reported that a dynamo which he had purchased for his cycle had vanished. A search was made of every desk in that room, and the missing article was discovered in BLANK's desk. We have found the thief. BLANK, you will leave the school immediately and don't come back." The culprit made his way through the assembled school and, after a short interval, we were told to go back to our classrooms. In retrospect, I admire the way in which the Head handled a most unpleasant task with the firmness that the occasion demanded. During the remaining four terms that I was at the school, pilfering was unknown.

Some ten days after Whitsun, the country had a General Election on May 30th, the first for almost five years. With several of my friends I had an interesting ten days or so attending the various political meetings and thoroughly enjoying the invariable Question Time, when there always seemed to be someone from the opposition ready to discomfit the candidate. It was a three-cornered fight. Once again, Mr Hugh Morrison, the retiring Member, represented the Conservative cause and tradition was followed when he addressed a packed eve-of-poll meeting in the Market House (now the library).

Charlie Rose and I went along to see and hear the fun, which was followed by a march to the White Hart Hotel where Mr Morrison addressed the crowd from the balcony. We saw "Tarzan" Taylor, one of our masters, watching us and next morning both Charlie and I received "impots" from him as we had not completed the homework which he had set. He rightly pointed out that we had had time to attend political meetings so we should have found time to complete our homework.

The local result was another victory for the Conservatives. At a national level, the Labour party, while winning most seats did not have an overall majority. They did, however, manage to remain in office, under Mr Ramsey MacDonald, for almost two-and-a-half years.

On the first Wednesday in June we all had to attend the Area Sports held at Victoria Park. That summer had been fairly good weather-wise, but that afternoon proved an exception for we had torrential rain. Charlie Rose and I were lucky enough to be near the large marquee, so we dashed in there just after our arrival and waited for the downpour to cease. Most of the teachers had done likewise and I remember our new headmaster climbing on to a trestle table to chair a very impromptu meeting which decided to postpone the event. We started to make our way home. By this time the rain was down to a very fine drizzle and our timing was quite perfect, for we arrived in the Market Place just in time to hear a broadcast of the Derby from a loudspeaker van. Today, such a thing would be quite commonplace. At that time it was magic. The van belonged to Western Wireless, which had a shop in Fisherton Street. Almost before the race started, it seemed to be over and it was won by a rank outsider called Trigo.

I was playing cricket at the nets in the School Field one evening when "Fuzzy" Richards called me to ask if I would stand as umpire in a junior House match that was about to commence between Trelawny and Wolsey. Although this was somewhat of a mis-match, between a very strong side and much weaker opponents, no-one could have anticipated the result. The Trelawny captain, Bob Masters (still wearing the scar from the beamer that I had bowled at him some two years earlier), opened the innings and was soon knocking boundaries to all parts of the field. When a halt was called for bad light the team had amassed well over 150 runs and his personal contribution was 116 not out. The Wolsey innings the following evening was quite a shambles, with no less than ten players getting ducks, most of them clean bowled. Bob Masters came out with a bowling analysis of five wickets for one run but even that was trumped by Banks with five for none, a remarkable performance and one which surely should be in the Guinness Book of Records.

After leaving school, Bob joined Southampton City Police as a constable and worked his way up to deputy chief constable. Strangely, my form of that year held two more policemen of the future — Eddie Noble, who became a chief superintendent in the Wiltshire County Constabulary and Len Moore who became an inspector in the same force. One other of our colleagues unfortunately went in the opposite direction and spent time in prison — he was even as a boy blessed with too much charm, which was to prove his downfall.

Right throughout that school year, I had been putting my new-found interest in the art of lettering to good use. Wherever possible, I tried my hand — history, English and geography essays began to acquire new and sometimes (dare I say) appropriate headings. I remember one history essay in particular. It was on the Magna Carta. Not only did I use Old English for the title but also had the temerity to try to copy in facsimile the first three lines of that historic document. My reward from "Tich" Oram, the history master, was a right telling off for not spending more time on the mundane side of the composition. Nevertheless, I felt more and more that I would like to follow lettering as a career and, with this in mind, I went with my father to see Mr Faulkner, headmaster at the School of Art. He suggested that I should go along in the following September to enrol in the lettering and sign-writing classes. This meant that on three evenings I would have to attend between seven and nine o'clock. With one or two nights already booked for Scouts plus the usual homework, I was not left with much spare time.

I had hoped that, as in the previous year, I might be able to go and help at Farr's again during the summer holidays. It was not to be, because the firm was now on its last legs, with only four employees left of the twenty-odd who had been there only seven years earlier. It was a sad state of affairs brought about mainly by the death, in the early Twenties, of Mrs Farr a good businesswoman, and the disastrous fire of 1925. I therefore spent that holiday playing cricket and exploring South Wiltshire on my bike, armed with a sketch-book. In a way I suppose that I was somewhat of an enigma — I like art, which might have branded me a cissy by my friends had this idiosyncrasy not been somewhat offset by my fondness for sport. These days, fortunately, most people are tolerant of those males who find pleasure in the arts. In my boyhood it was looked on as non-macho by youngsters.

There was great excitement among my crowd when, in mid-August, Flight Lieutenant Waghorn, flying one of the Supermarine 56 Seaplanes which had been specially built for the Schneider Trophy race to be held in September, broke the air-speed record by exceeding 350 miles per hour. Our elders were more excited by an apparently mundane local announcement. Mr Tom Cook, who farmed at Bemerton, decided to start retailing milk. His new bright yellow painted vans were everywhere to be seen. I can remember the two front doors had "Milk, 5d a quart" in red lettering, which looked most distinctive against the yellow background. Why was this event of such importance? — just that every other retailer was charging sevenpence a quart. Dad and Mum decided to carry on with their old suppliers, Taylors of Alderbury and Musselwhite of Petersfinger. They each supplied a pint a day and had been doing so for years and Dad, especially, thought loyalty counted for something. Cook made severe inroads into his competitors' rounds — he had, of course, succeeded in cutting out the middleman.

On September 7th, I was fortunate indeed, when as an early

Part of the fleet of coaches which left the city heading for the Schneider Trophy race in 1929. Hundreds more spectators travelled by special trains laid on for the great occasion.

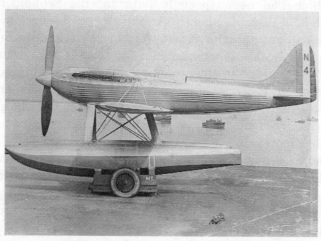

The Supermarine S6 — winner of the 1929 Schneider Trophy. Designed by R.J. Mitchell, who died at the early age of 37, it was the forerunner of the Spitfire which, with the Hurricane, enabled the Royal Air Force to win the Battle of Britain in 1940.

birthday present (my birthday was not until the 22nd) my sister and her boyfriend took me to see the Schneider Trophy Air Race. Great interest was shown by every paper and for weeks we had been reading of the capabilities of the rival teams. Great Britain, winners in Italy in 1927, hosted the competition and were opposed by a strong Italian team who had been given a great send-off by Mussolini — then at the height of his powers. We had on our side a strong team who were each flying the Supermarine 56a — which in many ways bore a resemblance to the later Spitfire. The race, for seaplanes only, was flown over a triangular course between the mainland and the Isle of Wight, roughly from Hayling Island to Bembridge and Stokes Bay, near Gosport.

We went by train from Salisbury to Gosport, where coaches, mostly privately owned, were waiting — the owners determined to make hay while the sun shone, as it most certainly did on that day. The driver of our coach could not have had a very profitable time, however. The coach, which I would think was built probably to carry about twenty passengers, must have had twice that number on board. The poor old thing slowly made its way, carrying this tremendous weight, towards Stokes Bay. When only about a quarter-mile from the beach, disaster struck, the nearside front tyre suddenly blew. The driver stopped, got down, had a look at the damage and suggested that everyone dismounted so that he could change the wheel. I felt sorry for that man for the response was quite frightening, had he insisted in his request he might have been lynched. The net result was that he resumed his seat, started the engine and the coach literally wobbled slowly to its destination. When we got down, I went with Phil (who eventually became my brother-in-law) to have a look at the damage. The tyre had been cut to ribbons and the wheel looked a decidedly funny shape. One can only hope that the driver was able to do enough journeys that day to enable him to pay a considerable bill.

In these days when times and results are flashed across the world in the twinkling of an eyelid, it seems incredible that only just over sixty years ago the method used to tell the assembled thousands of people the race times was large result boards, some fifteen feet square, which had been erected at various vantage points. These had been prepared as a grid: on the left were the names and nationalities of the pilots and along the top were headings for laps one, two and three. Under each lap number were two columns for time taken and average speed. A sign-writer was waiting in readiness by each board and the times were received by a phone installed some 100 yards away. From here a runner made the journey and handed the details to the writer, who then mounted a ladder and laboriously painted the numbers in characters some three inches high. The delay was frustrating to say the least. However, throughout a long and hot afternoon, the craftsman responsible for the Stokes Bay result board, did not, despite the constant catcalls from the enormous crowd to speed up, at any time drop his standards.

The British seaplanes looked very futuristic in their silver and blue livery while the Italians in bright scarlet reminded one of Red Devils. Signor Mussolini had promised his pilots the very earth if they won, for winning meant much more than prestige, it was the "Open Sesame" to enormous sales to countries around the world. The Supermarine 56a had been designed by a genius, R.J. Mitchell (later of Spitfire fame) and was powered by Rolls-Royce engines. There is no doubt that the Spitfire evolved as a result of experience gained from the British entries for this 1929 race.

Every newspaper had for weeks been filled with stories of the forthcoming event and this resulted in almost two million people watching the race. This enormous crowd was augmented by almost every owner of a radio set as the BBC had done their best to provide worthwhile commentaries. The three British pilots: Flight Lieutenants Waghorn, Atcherly and D'Arcy Grieg, were known in every home. Waghorn was looked upon as the most consistent, while Atcherly had the reputation of a daredevil. One of his contemporaries recently told me "the man was mad as a bloody hatter". (He went on to become Air-Marshal Atcherly). The race result was to prove the accuracy of the newspapers' prognostications.

The first competitor was Flight Lieutenant Waghorn, who had thrilled the country during the previous month when he had clocked up a new air speed world record of 350mph. His first lap resulted in an average speed of 300mph and his consistency was shown when he returned almost identical figures for each succeeding lap. This was an amazing speed for 1929 and produced an exciting spectacle. We were fortunate in being right opposite the marking buoy, half a mile out to sea from the beach.

The technique used by each of the six pilots was the same. They flew along the straight at about one thousand feet, dived to two hundred as they banked right to round the marker buoy and then climbed steeply to resume their original height. As each side of the triangular course was only about twelve miles, when one considers the loss of speed when making quite sharp turns, the average speeds were quite fantastic. After all it was only twenty five years earlier that the Wright Brothers had made the first powered flight. Waghorn's fastest lap showed an average of 303mph and this proved to be beyond the rest. Only one Italian finished the race and Atcherly really lived up to his reputation by clocking a faster time on his first circuit only to be disqualified because he had cut inside one of the marking buoys.

It truly was a day to remember, even though getting home again with so many others having the same idea, was far from easy. It made the crowd of 100,000 attending the Cup Final pale into insignificance. In the event this was the last Schneider Trophy race. Other countries just gave up the ghost — so that all Great Britain had to do in 1931 was to fly over the course and the trophy became hers for keeps as the winner on three successive occasions.

On the following Monday, I attended the Art School for the first time and for the next two years I was given a thorough grounding in Roman lettering. At times the subject was boring, but in later life, I've always been grateful for that training. Each Tuesday and Thursday I went into the class devoted to sign-writing although one corner of the room was given over to graining and marbling, which was still in vogue at that time.

The three students taking the latter subjects were somewhat older than the rest of us. Our first feeble steps in the craft were practice on boards some eight or ten feet in length, which were fixed on stands at a working height about five feet from the floor. These were painted black and the work we produced was washed off with a turpentine soaked rag and repainted before we left for home. I expect it was so bad that obliteration was the best treatment for it. After a few weeks, we were promoted to producing individual signs, which prior to writing had been given some six coats of paint. Between each coat the boards were rubbed down with pumice stone so that the final result was a beautifully smooth finish which looked like glass. We all had to supply our own palettes, two tin dippers — these were about the size of egg cups, held the paint and clipped on to the edge of the palette — and a mahl-stick. Mr Martin, our instructor, told us to send to Wrights of Lymm for three sign-writing pencils. These were sable brushes but woe betide anyone who called them that in front of Mr Martin, who was a first class craftsman. Like so many trades it had its own language to fox the uninitiated. Those evenings were very pleasant and I made some good friends. Few youngsters of today would want to spend years learning the trade but it was all worthwhile in the end.

The first House soccer match of the new season produced an indelible memory of horror for me. Although I preferred playing as an inside-forward, I was asked by our captain, Freddie Fulford to play at left-half against Dunstan House. Not many minutes into the game, one of their forwards burst through. George Woolnough, our goalkeeper, made a dash out to try and save but the ball went past him and was on its way towards the net. I made a mad sprint and endeavoured to boot the ball clear, but I sliced the kick and shot it beautifully into the goal. Ruefully, I apologised to our captain: "Sorry Freddie." Although he was hardly seventeen, he must have been old beyond his years because he said: "Don't worry, you did your best, the ball was going in anyway." Freddie is still a good friend sixty years later.

One morning, we were all chatting in the main playground waiting for the bell to summon us to Chapel. This usually sounded at about ten minutes to nine, thus allowing prefects time to mark the register. On this occasion no bell rang. At precisely nine o'clock, "Happy" the Head, came across the road from his house at Bishopsgate, mortar board on head, gown flapping and somewhat aghast when he saw we were all still in the playground. "What is happening?" — "Bell hasn't rung, Sir." — "Why not?" — "Won't work, Sir."

He ordered us to Chapel, while the caretaker was told to discover why the bell wouldn't ring. He climbed into the belfry and found that a soccer jersey had been threaded through the bell-rope just above the hole through which it went into the lobby, thus making it impossible to pull it down. The perpetrator was a practical joker in our form, Henry ("Willie") Wilson from Hindon, who in later life was to become a much respected headmaster himself.

At this time speed must have become very important in my life, because I remember asking if I could have a "Services" wrist watch for my Christmas present. The firm making the watch had targeted their advertising towards my age group and it showed the railway engine *The Flying Scotsman* as it started its record breaking run from London to Edinburgh. Strapped to one of the driving wheels was a Services watch, which according to the railway officials kept perfect time despite the terrific pounding which it had encountered during its 400-odd-mile journey. The ad must have sold thousands of watches — mine had only a short life of less than a year and when I took it for repair to the most reputable jeweller where it had been purchased, was told that it was not worth mending.

The school play that year was written by the headmaster. Called *A Man born to be King* it was excellent and attracted large audiences to the performances at the Victoria Hall in Rollestone Street. The hall, a late Victorian building, had had a somewhat chequered life. Originally built as a swimming bath, in winter it became a hall seating between four hundred and five hundred people and for many years was a popular venue for all types of entertainment. Just after the outbreak of the Second World War it was commandeered by the Army. In 1942 the hall became the city's British Restaurant and continued as such until 1950. A restaurateur from the Isle of Wight then ran it as a private cafe, but his venture was short-lived and, from 1952, Victoria Hall became a printing works for the next thirty-eight years.

One evening during the week before Christmas, Dad had a visit from Mr Frank Crebo, who had worked with him at Farr's in the years prior to the Great War. He came with the offer of a job — he was foreman at Heaver's of Durrington, which at that time employed some forty men. As I wrote earlier, Farr's was no longer the thriving business of the early twenties and Mr Frank Farr was ill (he died a few months later), so Dad was glad of the opportunity. There was, however, a lot of heart-searching before a decision was made. For one thing, Durrington was eleven miles from Salisbury.

This meant leaving the Market Place at seven each morning and returning at half past eight each evening — on Saturdays he would be home by half past two. In all, away for seventy five hours, plus the walk to and from the market.

Transport direct from the Market Place to Heaver's works was provided by a Mr Hawkins from Durrington, who was running a fourteen-seater coach for which a weekly workman's ticket cost ten shillings and sixpence. Heaver's seemed to be flourishing, with a full order book. Good wages were paid plus overtime if anyone wanted it. (I shouldn't think many had the strength in view of the normal working week). Dad accepted the job. Mr Farr was most upset and decided the time had come to cease trading. The other three employees managed to find work, so that was the end of a business which stretched back well over a hundred years.

In celebration of the new job, Dad decided to purchase a radio, which was installed on Christmas Eve. It was a four-valve Marconiphone with a separate speaker in a square case. We had to erect an aerial and Dad procured some two-inch steel piping about twenty feet in length which was sunk some three feet into concrete at the bottom of the garden. The aerial consisted of two parallel insulated wires some thirty five feet long and kept three feet apart by battens. One of these battens was attached to the metal pole, the other fixed to the window sill of the top bedroom. From the two wires went a lead — into an ebonite tube which went through the kitchen window sill. Reception in those days seemed to be affected greatly by the efficiency or otherwise of the aerial. We must have done a good job because the set worked perfectly and a new era of family entertainment had dawned.

The BBC in those days was very stuffy, especially on Sundays, when broadcasting had to be of a suitable nature for the day of rest. No transmissions were allowed before 3.30pm and then they started with performances of Bach Cantatas, week after week. The stuffiness can be imagined when one considers that male news-readers, unseen by any audience, were forced to wear evening dress. How times have changed.

Chapter Four 1930
I start earning a living

The 1930s really did come in like a lion, for on a Sunday evening early in January Britain was hit by a 100-mile-an-hour hurricane. I was fifteen and thought myself no end of a man, but that night was terrifying, it was impossible to sleep. All night long we heard sounds of slates and tiles smashing to the ground so that it seemed it was only a matter of time before the roof was blown off. That night, I was sleeping in the top room, on the second storey, immediately under that roof and I remember how I shivered because I really was scared. The night seemed endless but towards dawn the storm abated and at first light I looked out towards the Cathedral, for I was quite sure the spire must have been a casualty, but there it was standing as proudly as ever. It was a different story for many beautiful old trees. The Waterloo elms in the South West corner of the Close were uprooted, the lovely beeches on the Wilton Road between Skew Bridge and the Park wall, which had made such a wonderful avenue, had become victims. It took three months to clear the road, even though several firms of timber merchants were working from daylight to dark — but it should be remembered they had no chain saws.

In the town it was amazing how little structural damage had been done. I would rate the storm as at least the equal of that experienced locally on Thursday, January 25th 1990, sixty years later. My mother and father said that they had never seen anything like it and they were born in the early 1880s. Some trees blown down in the countryside were never cleared, and just stayed where they had fallen until they rotted away. Twenty six people lost their lives in that dreadful night. I remember that the Wilton boys who came to school by bus had to take a detour via Quidhampton for most of that term and used it as an excuse for constant lateness.

During the spring term of 1930, our form room was on the second floor of the main school building, overlooking the Bishop's Palace kitchen gardens, and I was fortunate enough to have bagged a desk in the back row, right by the window. We had a cold spell for many weeks, so cold that a flock of seagulls could be seen in the garden scrounging for food, to the great dismay of the head gardener and his army of underlings. Over the grapevine we heard that their task was made much harder because of the Bishop's attitude — he refused to have any killed — but I expect he still thought the poor chaps should produce winter and spring greens!

At around this time the city was shaken to the core when a firm of multiple tailors purchased the premises where George Hill carried on the China and Glass business by the Poultry Cross. Just after the building was demolished, the company wrote to the City Council asking that the ancient cross should be moved to a more suitable site as it was a restriction on trade. There was an immediate furore and the story was splashed across the national newspapers. Looking back, I have no doubt that the letter was written with tongue in cheek, as the resulting free publicity was worth a great deal of money. The local populace never bore the company ill-will for the shop was successful from the outset, due, no doubt, to the wonderful value that was offered. A three-piece made-to-measure suit in excellent material cost only 37s 6d. A perfect fit was guaranteed, as was the delivery time of only fourteen days. In the case of bereavement, they guaranteed a mourning suit would be delivered in three days. Service indeed.

On Easter Monday, our Scout troop made one of many wonderful visits to Winterbourne Gunner. A very friendly farmer allowed us to camp on his land and gave us full rein to use any wood we wanted from a quite large coppice. The site available was downland with a valley running through and some three square miles in area. It was ideal territory and we made full use of our opportunities to practice scoutcraft.

At about this time, a young unknown London secretary suddenly became world famous and her name, Amy Johnson, was on everyone's lips. Flying a secondhand Gypsy Moth she reached Australia less than three weeks after leaving London. It was an incredible feat and soon we were all singing the hit song of that summer — "Amy, wonderful Amy".

On the first Saturday of the new cricket season, School played Andover Grammar at Andover and the game produced a remarkable performance. Jack Harrison not only made a century but also took five of the opponents' wickets — a feat that brought him the weekly prize of the Jack Hobbs' bat from *The Star*, a national evening newspaper, for outstanding performance in school cricket. The following Thursday was Ascension Day, when the annual match between School and the Masters was played. Jack followed his century of the previous Saturday by knocking up eighty-odd not out but I was not there to see it. Attendance by the whole school at the match was compulsory, but Ascension Day was also the day of Salisbury Races. Three of us had never been to the racecourse, so as soon as the register had been marked at the school field we made our way to Mrs Bedford's garden right by the pavilion.

The Bedfords had a greengrocery shop in Fish Row and possessed a fair-sized garden where the produce was grown. All members of the family were tiny — well under five feet — and as a profitable sideline they made use of their close vicinity to the school field and sold sweets and mineral waters at the back door, just out of sight from the pavilion and well screened by hedges. We passed the back door, went round the path to the front and so to the road, where we had left our bikes in readiness. Quickly off came our school caps and we were on our way to the Racecourse. By the time we arrived only two races remained to be run, we saw the horses as they flashed by our vantage point on the free part of the course, which must have been all of a quarter of a mile from the finishing post. It was hardly worth all the bother and I remember that we made our way home by a very circuitous route to avoid the school field. I was at school early on the following day to check up on the scores of the previous day's match in case I was asked. In the event we were never missed, though for a few days we were looked upon by our colleagues as gay dogs — but not one of them split on us.

On Whit Saturday, we had a County Scout Parade in the grounds of Marlborough College, when the Chief Scout, Lord Baden Powell was present. B.P. as he was affectionately known, had been one of my boyhood heroes ever since my enrollment into the Cubs.

We had to meet at our troop headquarters in Gigant Street. When we got there it was absolutely tipping down with rain and we had to wait in the street as the door was locked and there was no sign of our Scoutmaster, the Reverend Plaxton. Presently his wife arrived, they had only been married a few months, asked for me, told me that her husband was ill and asked me to take command. Mr Plaxton had written me a note giving instructions for the day, so there I was, at fifteen, with twenty odd scouts in my care.

I lined them up and off we marched to the District HQ in Castle Street, where coaches were waiting. The route I followed was via the side streets, my confidence was not high. When we reached Castle Street, I told the District Commissioner, Mr P.J. Southon, what had happened, expecting him to take over, but he just said "Carry on". One or two in our troop took the mickey, but the majority were real trumps and obeyed orders. During the afternoon we lined up rather like the spokes of a wheel, fifty scouts in each line, and B.P. walked round the inner circle and inspected us. I was heading one of the lines and actually met my hero. He was quite a tiny man, very intense — hardly the picture of a Major General, the hero of Mafeking during the Boer War, but I felt there was something of an aura about him. Sixty odd years on, I feel that I was lucky to meet one of the greatest men of his time.

After the debacle of 1928, the Scouts Grose Trophy competition had been moved from Easter to Whitsun and, as far as 1930 was concerned, the move certainly paid off, for Whit Monday was a truly glorious day. We (several hundred of us) took the Bournemouth train to Alderbury Junction, which had just a simple platform on each side of the track. From there we marched through beautiful countryside for a mile or so and then came to a plantation of Norwegian spruce. At least it had been a plantation, some half a mile square, but the great storm of January had brought down every tree. We halted and were met by the Earl of Radnor's heir, Lord Folkestone, the District Commissioner, Mr P.J. Southon, and "Wacker" Chaplin, the Scout treasurer and a keen photographer. Lord Folkestone told us we could cut any timber we wanted and Mr Southon had produced sketches of various types of bivouacs to show us what was needed for the competition. Mr Chaplin, I remember, said the devastation reminded him of the Western Front in the First World War. We split up into patrols, it was a wonderful day, hot enough to cause the resin in the trees to become sticky — I can still recall the smell. Although our axes were blunt, we went to it with a will, measuring the logs by means of our Scout staves, which were calibrated in feet and inches. By mid-afternoon everyone had a presentable dwelling — each patrol had been given a large ball of twine so our knot skills were brought into use — and finally the roof was thatched with bracken. As we had time left over, ours was furnished with two beds made from logs, with bracken mattresses. It was all good fun and the sun was still really hot as we marched back to the Junction Halt.

What a difference twenty four hours can make. I had arranged with two Scout friends to go off on the following day to cycle to Milford-on-Sea and camp until Friday. Tuesday dawned quite cold but dry. We started away at about nine o'clock and despite our loaded cycles made good time to reach Milford by midday. As we had only taken a small patrol tent made for two the next three days were a bit of a squash, but this helped to keep us warm at night. Our two blankets apiece made into sleeping bags with large blanket pins were inadequate for what turned out to be a quite cold snap. It was almost too cold to go on to the beach and we spent our small amount of pocket money on magazines and newspapers, which we read from cover to cover. When Friday came round, I think we were all pleased to make our way home, but in manly fashion we none of us gave away our true feelings.

The following weekend, another patrol leader and myself did our First Class hike. We had to carry enough food for thirty hours, a tent, but NO compass or watch, and we had to complete a round trip of fifteen miles on foot. We set out on a Saturday afternoon that was quite warm. After a mile or two it was very warm, the packs were heavy and our uniforms hot. Gradually we made our way to the camp site at Winterbourne and arrived there at about five o'clock, pitched tent, gathered some wood, got a fire going and had tea. We then went for a mooch around. That area, although only a few miles from Salisbury and Amesbury, was quite deserted, so we saw no-one. Back to the tent, supper and so to bed. I don't suppose either of us needed much rocking. We were awakened by the sun streaming into the tent, so we went to the cow trough and washed, then back, lit the fire and enjoyed breakfast. Remember, we had no watches! After breakfast, a walk to the nearby ruined windmill, which had probably not changed in a hundred years, the machinery being on the floor where it had crashed. After playing around there for some time we went back to the tent, made up the fire and cooked our dinner of sausages and chips. When we had eaten this, we went for another stroll and soon it seemed time for tea. After tea, another walk and we decided between us that it must be between six and seven o'clock and it would soon be time to pack up and make our way back to Salisbury. Just then we met a man walking and we cheated when we asked him if he could tell us the time. I have never been so dumbfounded as when he replied: "Nearly a quarter to twelve." Heaven knows at what time we had got up that morning. We were now in a bit of a predicament as we had eaten all our food, so we decided to call it a day, pack up and do the test all over again on another weekend. The journey back to

"Auntie Smiler", the star of the Salisbury Infirmary Carnival in 1930. As she pedalled her way around the city, Auntie turned her head from side to side as though acknowledging the cheering crowds.

Salisbury seemed endless and as we knew that we had failed the test, when a bus came along we caught it and did the last three miles in comfort.

In the middle of that summer term, my last at school, Salisbury had a carnival. This was held to raise money for an extension to the Infirmary, which included adding another storey to the main building. The Mayor, Cllr H.B. Medway, a tailor from Winchester Street, chaired the appeal and was a most enthusiastic leader. A niece of the Earl of Pembroke, Miss Gwendolyn Wilkinson, became a very stately Carnival Queen and she was attended by six maids of honour. We had a collection at school and the Carnival Queen, with her retinue paid a visit to collect the proceeds. The entire school lined up in the playground, the presentation to the queen being made by the head boy, Ham Robinson (his initials were H.A.M.), who made a short speech with a face that, in the presence of the beautiful females, grew more red by the minute.

The procession on the Wednesday evening was a splendid affair but I remember the outstanding entry was "Auntie Smiler" — a nurse some twelve or fifteen feet in height who pedalled blissfully on her way, pushing an open Baby Austin Seven. As she pedalled she turned her head from side to side. Two Salisbury business men, Mr J. Scholfield of the Salisbury Steam Laundry and Mr "Wiggy" Harris of Goddards Garage, were the inventors of "Auntie" — a wonderful effort. This was the first carnival the city had had for many a long year and unfortunately it was to be another twenty odd before the next one.

In July, my father had to pay a visit to Captain (as he still styled himself) Happold to tell him that I would be leaving at the end of the term. Dad had arranged with Mr Harry Martin, the sign-writer, that I would start work with him in August. When the Head heard what I intended to do he became quite upset and said his boys did not go in for that sort of work, they looked for something better. As far as I could make out they had a bit of an argument and Dad came home with the impression that the Head was an out and out snob. For myself, I see no wrong in any job of work that is honest — we are all made differently and I think the great thing is that one should get happiness and satisfaction from one's labours.

On a Friday evening towards the end of the month, Mr Aubrey

Searle came to ask if I would like to play for the St Martin's Cricket Team the following day. The occasion was a Salisbury and District League match against Norman Court at Shady Bower. I did not need to be asked twice as it had always been my ambition to play for the Saints. This opportunity had only come about as one of the regulars had had to cry off at the last moment and I had been keen in the nets that were held each Thursday evening.

Strangely, although I was excited, Dad was even more so, and for the first time for many years, cricket was more important than his allotment. In the event I did not have a great deal to do. We won the toss, batted first and with good scores from our early batsmen, the innings was declared long before it was my turn to bat. The Saints' bowling was first class, and thanks to Aubrey Searle, Len Brown and Jack Mussell, the Norman Court team were soon all out for under forty runs. They followed on, still sixty odd behind, and wickets soon started falling again. Len Brown, an all round sportsman (he played in goal for Salisbury City and Wiltshire as well as being table tennis champion) was a really fast left-hand bowler, putting all his thirteen or so stones into every delivery. That afternoon, I was fielding at second slip and during the visitors' second innings, one of Len Brown's specials spreadeagled the stumps. Then we couldn't find one of the bails and it was several minutes before a shout went up of "Here it is". It was so far from the broken wicket that the umpires decided to measure the distance, which proved to be 36 yards. I've often wondered just how fast Len Brown's bowling really was!

Almost as soon as the term finished, I was off to a Scout camp at Milford-on-Sea and had charge of a patrol from our troop, which was now under the command of the Curate, the Reverend C.A. Plaxton (later Archdeacon of Wiltshire). We went by train to Southampton, changed there for New Milton, where "Placko" was waiting with his bull-nosed Morris three-seater to ferry the six of us, with equipment, to the camp site some four miles away.

The camp was run each year by the Reverend Dr Hawes of Salisbury Theological College, and consisted that year of three patrols — one from 12th Holborn (London), one from 1st Hendon and ourselves. The emphasis was on smartness and points were awarded throughout the ten days spent there. It was real spit and polish — at inspection each morning all kit had to be laid out in true Army fashion, tent walls neatly rolled up, and we had to stand rigidly to attention all the while inspection was made. It was great fun and we loved the competition.

However, we got off to a terrible start. For months we had been screwing and scraping to raise the sum of two pounds ten shillings, with which to purchase a secondhand bell tent. In 1930, equipment from the First World War was still readily available and our choice was a pale green USA issue bell tent, complete with all accessories. Delivery of this was only made a couple of days before our departure for camp, so we had no time to pitch it and make sure everything was in order. As soon as we arrived at the camp site we set to — got the tent from its canvas bag and proceeded to erect it, all the time under the watchful eye of Dr Hawes and his assistants. The tent looked a good job but had one great drawback. It was covered in the names (written with indelible purple pencils) of the GIs who had used it all those years before. Some of the scribblings were quite funny — none, fortunately, were filthy, but I remember one which read "Spud Murphy commonly known as Stew Bum". Imagine our horror, but we need not have worried — the writings were totally ignored by the officers.

One other moment of horror from that camp comes to mind —the day that I tore my navy blue serge shorts. I had no spare pair so what to do? We went to the nearest corner shop — my shorts being held together with several safety pins — and there I purchased a packet of needles and some cotton, but unfortunately the lady only had white. Back to the camp and I then spent quite some time on the repair, which when finished did not look too bad (to my eyes), but the white cotton on navy blue ground drew attention to the tear. Then inspiration struck — the hedge at the side of the field was full of blackberries, so off I went, got quite a lot of these and squeezed the juice on the cotton which turned a lovely shade of purply-blue. When I arrived home the family had a good laugh at my predicament and an even bigger one at my attempt to overcome it.

I remember that in the 12th Holborn Patrol there were two German brothers whose father worked in the German Embassy.

They were a friendly pair and I've often wondered what happened to them when war started just nine years later.

When I got home, I was met with the news that owing to a turn-down in trade, Mr Harry Martin no longer needed my services. I still wanted to follow a lettering career so made the rounds of the other sign-writers, Mr Dudley Jennings, Mr Tommy Haynes and Haynes and Son. The answer was the same everywhere, trade was bad but they would take my name and if anything came up ... After a few weeks, I began to look at other occupations but jobs were few and far between. Several of my former schoolmates were still looking the following spring. It was the beginning of the depression that had hit the USA a couple of years earlier. At the end of August there was a sign outside Tommy Sparks, the Milford Street hairdresser, which read "Apprentice required". I went home and told Mum but she was against me trying for the job — I'm glad I didn't for I think I would have hated it.

The weeks seemed to fly by and then one Monday in September I saw some new posters being put up on the walls above the Empire Meat Company in Ox Row at the side of the Market Place. One side of the two bay windows read "Posters" and the other "Showcards". I didn't even know the place called Empire Studios existed. Later that Monday morning, after a discussion with Mum, I went to see if they had a vacancy. Mr C.B. Gething, the owner, said that he had thought about taking an indentured apprentice but would require a premium. This dashed my hopes for I knew my parents could not afford it, but Mum once again came up with the answer and took me along to Jonas and Parker, solicitors to the Charity of John, Duke of Somerset. Through the generosity of this eighteenth century gentleman, sufficient funds were available each year to apprentice some ten poor children who must be natives of the city parishes of St Martin, St Edmund or St Thomas. They took all the details and I was given some forms to take to Mr Gething. I started work with him on October 2nd, on a purely temporary basis, and eventually the indentures were signed during the first week of December. My wages during the first year were to be seven shillings and sixpence, fifteen shillings in the second and one pound in the third and final year. After payment of one shilling and two pence for the National Health and Unemployment stamp, my take-home pay was six shillings and fourpence. The indenture bound me not to contract matrimony and not to frequent gaming houses or houses of ill-repute during my apprenticeship. Even had I wanted to do these things the shortage of money would have stopped me.

The six shillings and fourpence that I collected each week was handed over to my mother, who put two shillings and sixpence into a fund for my clothes. I got one shilling and fourpence while she retained the other half-a-crown for my keep. I think that I was lucky to have parents who taught me the value of money. These days, far too many youngsters are spoilt by their parents, with the result that when the time comes to leave home they have no idea of how to cope.

On Sunday, October 5th I went to church in the morning as usual. On coming out from the service at 12.30pm I heard a shout that was unique — a newsvendor bawling "R101 crashes. Special Edition". *The People* must have really gone to it to produce that paper to record the tragedy that had occurred during the previous night. The airship R101 was the successor to the R100, Britain's most successful dirigible, designed by that great engineer Barnes Wallis (later of Dambusters fame). On the Saturday evening, it had set out from Cardington for India and included in the passenger list was the Secretary for Air, Lord Thomson. It was a foolhardy attempt because the R101, which had suffered many teething problems, crashed on a hillside at Beauvais in France, exploding like a fireball. The death toll was forty four. There were only eight survivors. This was the only occasion in my life that I can recall the production of a special edition of a newspaper on the Sabbath. The tragedy shocked the nation, for the R101 was thought to be the way forward for air travel, but the crash meant the end of airship manufacture in this country.

One little memory of my early days at work is of the fair, held on the third Monday of October each year. Working as I did in Ox Row, which is on the south side of the market, the fair was just outside the window of the main studio and created a three-day diversion. Just after nine o'clock the men started to arrive to order price cards, and something that happened that first morning stood me in good stead for the rest of my business career. I learned never, ever, to take down a customer's copy without getting him to countersign what I had written.

The reason for this instruction was that Mr Gething's other assistant had taken down the copy dictated by the owner of a fair ride, a mistake was made, six cards were produced by hand and three hours' work was wasted. It was quite useless to tell the man that he must have dictated the wrong price, if you take down a customer's copy then you are on a hiding to nothing.

As I was attending the Art School on both the Monday and Tuesday evenings of that week, I made the most of wandering around the fair at lunchtime. On the Tuesday, I had one silver shilling in the world and changed this for twelve pennies at a circular stall called "roll-a-penny". You placed a penny at the top of a groove and off in a sloping channel it went, down on to a table having bell pushes all over it. If the penny landed on a push (which was about half-an-inch in diameter) a bell rang and a light came on in a sign which indicated how much you had won — the reward rising from a free go up to twelve pence or one shilling. I had a go, no luck, another go, no luck, and soon was left with only one penny. Disconsolately I wandered off back to work. The next lunchtime, the fair once again cast its magnetic attraction. Once again, I found myself back at the same roll-a-penny stall and thought I would have one more try. Off my last penny went and rolled almost as far as it could go, fell over, and a bell rang. At the same moment a light was flashing on the prize chart. I had won a shilling. The owner paid me out in coppers, they went straight into my pocket and I don't think I've rolled-a-penny in all the years since that lunchtime.

Although I had left school and consequently was relieved of the nightly chore of homework, I had little spare time. Monday and Tuesday evenings were still taken up by attending Art School, Wednesday was Scout Parade, Thursday, Art School again and on Fridays we had a small club at the Lear Memorial Rooms in Gigant Street. This was run for those attending the Sunday afternoon Bible Class and, though it was sadly short of equipment, provided an excellent evening's entertainment. We had a table-tennis table, a small quarter-sized billiard table, bar skittles and that was about the sum total. The club was for boys only, girls met on a separate night; even their Bible Class was held at a different venue. It would have been much greater fun if we had been allowed to mix, but in those days there were too many Mrs Grundys saying "no" to everything. We all worked on Saturday mornings, leaving off at one o'clock after receiving our pay. That year, I was playing football for St Martin's Boys. This, too, was run in connection with the Bible Class and we had a full fixture list of friendly matches. These were against other youth teams from St Mark's, St Edmund's, St Thomas's, St Paul's, Bemerton, the Salisbury Boys' Club, St Francis (this was a new parish, having been formed in 1928, for which the Vicar, the Reverend Mauleverer, regularly turned out), Wilton Boys, and Amesbury Boys. Although termed "friendly" games, they were very competitive and there was a great deal of rivalry.

We spent our Saturday evenings mooching around the Market and in and out of Woolworth's. This really was a period of growing up, few of us needed to shave more than once a week, our hair (every hair) was kept in place with the aid of Field's Lavender Solidified Brilliantine, purchased for threepence a tin at Woolworth's toiletries counter. Our mothers were always complaining about the greasy marks left on pillowcases. The trademark of male youth at that time was the wearing of white silk scarves.

Most of us had to be home at the time stated by our parents, who would brook no argument. My time was half past nine and I kept to it. On one occasion, when I was delayed by a heated discussion on football so forgot the time, my father came to look for me at ten o'clock and I suffered a real wigging. If we were in funds on a Saturday evening, we would go to the pictures, a front seat cost us fourpence, and after the show went to Prewetts fish and chip shop in Milford Street, where we could buy a piece of cod for twopence and a pennyworth of chips. This was served on a plate and as we sat eating away at one of the marble topped tables, our white silk scarves around our necks, our hair plastered with solid brilliantine, we behaved with as much aplomb as the film stars we had just seen dining in dress suits.

Sunday was still looked on as a day apart. We had to wear our best suits which were always well brushed. Off we went to church in the morning, Bible Class in the vestry during the afternoon and church again in the evening. Usually three or four of us would go for a walk in late afternoon and again after church during the summer, but in winter we often made our way to the Salisbury Brotherhood meeting held in the Co-operative Hall in Winchester Street. These were usually of great interest consisting (besides the usual hymns and prayers) of talks and slide shows. I remember that at one of these Mr W.A.C. Chaplin (the "Wacker" of the Scout movement) showed part of a collection of photographs taken by him while he served at the front during the Great War. Looking back, what a dedicated photographer he must have been to bother to carry a camera around with him on the battlefield. At the end of the meeting, a free cup of tea was served which always seemed to taste better than that obtained at home.

One of the radio celebrities of this time was Christopher Stone, who played programmes of the latest gramophone records. His popularity stemmed from his wide choice which ranged from *The Laughing Policeman* to Mozart. On Christmas Day he presented a programme of three whole hours, which with his inimitable chatter between records was a memorable occasion. I suppose he was radio's first disc-jockey and to my mind has never been surpassed.

Chapter Five 1931
The year of depression

Early in January 1931, Salisbury was aghast when an SOS message was given over the radio at nine o'clock on a Sunday evening for a local girl who was missing. She was only fifteen years of age and both she and her family were quite well known to us. Apparently she had gone to work on the Saturday morning, returned home for her midday meal, gone back to work and had not been seen since the closure of the shop, a draper's in the city, that evening. Nothing more was heard of her, but later that week, rumours were rife in the town that her boyfriend, a sixteen-year-old assistant at a fish and chip shop who lived with his grandmother, was also missing. On the following Tuesday, ten days after their disappearance, the young couple were found by police at Yeovil, where they had been living as man and wife. They were brought back to Salisbury, the young man was charged and remanded on bail. He continued to work at the fish and chip shop and I imagine that the takings must have gone up over the next few months, as he had become something of a celebrity and people were anxious to have a look at this young blood.

In May, he appeared at the local Assizes and was sentenced to six months' imprisonment for the offence of "having carnal knowledge of a female below the age of sixteen years". I believe the relevant law is still on the statute book and it is perhaps as well that it is now not strictly adhered to, because our prisons would be even more crowded. The lady who let the young couple rooms at Yeovil was castigated by the judge, who said that she must have guessed their age but was only interested in monetary gain.

On another Sunday evening, a few weeks later, Salisbury was again mentioned on the nine o'clock news. It was announced that "Mr Hugh Morrison, the Member of Parliament for Salisbury, has

owing to ill-health accepted the office of Stewardship of the
Chiltern Hundreds. This will necessitate a by-election in the
constituency". It was all double-Dutch to me, but my mother
quickly explained that by accepting this office of profit under the
Crown, a Member of Parliament had to resign and that this was the
only way that it could be done. Another of our funny old British
customs! A week or so later, the local Conservative Association
chose a new candidate — Major J. Despencer-Robertson of Wilbury
House, near Cholderton. The Liberal Party once again relied upon
Mrs Masterman, the widow of a former Cabinet Minister, while Mr
Frank Hancock was in the Labour corner. There was all the usual
excitement of a by-election, with meetings addressed by Party big-
wigs, but now I seemed to be part of the action as I helped (in a
very minor way) to produce the usual crop of signs needed. I learnt
that business is accepted from all parties and framed canvas signs
stating Despencer-Robertson's Committee Rooms (in blue),
Masterman's Committee Rooms (in red) and Frank Hancock's
Committee Rooms (in red on a bright yellow ground) made their
way from Empire Studios in the Market Place for erection in
Catherine Street, Castle Street and Endless Street respectively.

It was expected that the result could be a close-run thing as Mrs
Masterman was a strong opponent for the new Conservative
candidate. Had she not given the late member, Mr Hugh Morrison,
a hard fight in 1929 and now she was up against untried opposition,
so who knows? It was generally thought that Mr Hancock stood
little chance — at that time the Labour Party was looked on by
Salisbury citizens as being not far removed from links with the
Kremlin!

We had all the usual eve-of-poll meetings — the Tories in the
Market House, the Liberals in the Victoria Hall and the Labour
Party in the Labour Hall in Endless Street. Voting took place as
usual on a Thursday and on Friday at one o'clock I was one of a
large crowd waiting outside the Guildhall for the result. As
expected, Mr Hancock languished way behind in third place but
Mrs Masterman had not done any better than in her previous
challenge of 1929 and Major J. Despencer-Robertson was elected as
Member, a position he was to hold for the next eleven years.

Easter of that year heralded the start of another depressingly wet summer. It rained heavily on each of the four days, through from Good Friday until Easter Monday. Although the three places of entertainment, the Palace, the Picture House and the New Theatre were not allowed to open on Good Friday, football was allowed at Victoria Park as long as the kick-off was delayed until after three o'clock. Salisbury City played on a muddy pitch on that day, but by Monday the Park was a quagmire. The city had an excellent team that year and picked up six Western League points from the three Easter games.

During early May, the Palace Theatre's life of almost forty two years came to an end. By this time the new Gaumont Palace was nearing completion on a site at the rear of the Canal and Catherine Street. Gaumont British also owned the Palace so decided to close the old theatre, which was originally built as the County Hall, rather than keep it open for a possibly unsuccessful summer season. It was rather an ironic decision, because just before the closure the Palace had enjoyed a profitable three months. This was due to the excellent Barry O'Brien Repertory Company, whose performances reached a very high standard, and as a result the theatre experienced a very late Indian Summer. Later that autumn the leading lady, Miss Nancy O'Neill, made her debut in films and during the next year or so was to be seen regularly at Salisbury's cinemas.

During the great storm of January 1930, the magnificent elm at Old Sarum, under which the Parliamentary elections for the Rotten Borough prior to 1831 were held, had been uprooted. The City Council decided that the spot should be marked and so on June 12, 1931, the former Prime Minister, the Rt Hon Stanley Baldwin, was invited to unveil a sarsen stone bearing a bronze plaque on the site. It was also decided to appoint the statesman a Freeman of the City and that the resolution should be inscribed on a vellum scroll, to be placed in a leather case, both to be embellished with the Coat of Arms. My employer, Mr C.B. Gething, was entrusted with the production of the scroll, which was beautifully written and illuminated. The capital letters were raised, then gilded with twenty four carat gold leaf. He also produced the Coat of Arms, which was incorporated into the leather case made by Mr Harry Bailey, the book-binder of Queen Street. The finished result was a piece of craftsmanship of which the city could be proud. Luckily the sun shone for the great occasion — I wonder how many people visit that Parliamentary Stone these days?

It was during June that my father began to suffer from stress caused by the long hours he had been working over the previous eighteen months. He had an outbreak of boils on his right posterior — a very unfortunate spot, as for some three weeks poor old Dad could not sit in a chair and had to spend day and night in bed, laying on his left side, not being able to turn over. The doctor called daily to lance the painful eruptions which fortunately vanished and he was able to resume work. At this time the recession meant he was working normal hours — a good thing, as I don't think he could have gone back to seventy plus hours a week for any length of time without a complete breakdown. He had been used to long hours in his younger days, but in 1931 he was approaching fifty and was too old for those capers.

Little cricket was possible that summer as three out of each four Saturdays were marred by rain, in any case St Martin's now only had a scratch team owing to the retirement through age of many former stalwarts. We only played friendly matches and I remember one of these versus Harnham, when I held three catches. I almost took a fourth, when Mr Robey, one of the opposing side, a very powerful hitter of the ball, pulled one round off the middle of the bat towards me, fielding some twenty five yards away at square leg. It was coming like a bullet, just above my head. I stuck up my hand, more in hope than anything else, and stopped it, but it didn't stick. I threw the ball in, my hand quite numb, and Teddy Bruton, our wicketkeeper, a friend of Dad's who was in his forties, came towards me and shouted for all to hear: "Young Maidment, if you get another one like that get out of the bloody way." That was the last season that St Martin's ran a team — a great pity after the fine reputation gained right through the Twenties.

At the end of June, Mr Gething's lease expired and he obtained rooms over the Co-operative Society's men's outfitting shop in Winchester Street. The move took three days and use was made of one of Mr Walter Gamblin's lorries. He had built up a business with daily runs to London. During this move, which was thirsty work, I went into a public house for the first time and was treated to a beer and lemon shandy. I remember that while we were there a message came through to Mr Gamblin that one of his vehicles had been involved in a collision in London and the lorry and driver were at a garage. He rang through, spoke to the garage manager and asked him to lend the driver sufficient funds to get a train back to Salisbury. That was how things were in 1931, few people had money in their pockets for emergencies.

The new premises had been empty for a year or so, after the death of the former owner, Mr Kington, who ran a brush and basket manufactory. There were still tools of the trade in the attics, including an overgrown pair of shears with blades about four feet in length, one of which was fixed at the end of a bench — presumably canes were placed on this and the other blade came down like a pair of giant scissors. Now that he had more space, Mr Gething started screen printing, which was then in its infancy, and it is amazing just how far the process has advanced in my lifetime. The first results were crude but from little acorns great oaks grow.

By this time the recession that had swept the United States some two years earlier was being felt in this country. Thanks to the advent of talking pictures, the world had suddenly become smaller. We now saw and heard events that had taken place on the other side of the world within a few days of their happening. For some time we had seen pictures of the frightening repercussions of the Wall Street crash, the lengthening queues in American cities as the workless waited patiently for the food that was being handed out by charities, and pictures of not so patient people going on the rampage to vent their frustration on whatever was to hand. This was the time of the song Brother can you spare a Dime. Now it seemed that this country was taking the same road — jobs were hard to come by. Those in permanent employment, such as railway workers, postmen, civil servants, and those working for local government, albeit in menial jobs, were looked upon as fortunate individuals. Salisbury was suffering rather less than most towns of a similar size because of the almost complete lack of manufacturing industries, while the presence of so many Army camps and Air Force stations in the vicinity brought welcome revenue.

To add to the gloom, that summer really was one of the wettest on record. It rained and it rained and it rained! Our Scout camp was to be held at Lee-on-Solent in late August and we all looked forward to what would have been a welcome break. As troop leader, I had spent many hours with the new Scoutmaster, Mr Hounsome, on the preparations. All food was on order, one of G. Mould and Sons' lorries was to transport us, and everyone had paid in their pound — the cost per head for a week. We were due to take off on the afternoon of Saturday, August 22nd, but on the previous Thursday, August 20th, we received a telegram from the Lee-on-Solent farmer who had agreed use of his site to say the field was under water. It was a terrible disappointment. The next day, at Mum's suggestion, I went to the railway station to inquire about the new Runabout tickets which had just been introduced. These enabled you to have unlimited travel within a restricted area at only ten shillings and sixpence for a week. It was wonderful value — especially as the ones operating from Salisbury included the line to Bournemouth and Weymouth.

As soon as I left work on Saturday, I dashed to the station and bought my ticket in readiness to start my holiday on Sunday, when the first train left for Bournemouth at about ten o'clock. Life did not seem quite so bad after all. I spoke too soon, for just after tea

The entrance to the Halle of John Halle just prior to the opening of the Gaumont Palace in 1931. The wooden scaffolding was some of the last to be used.

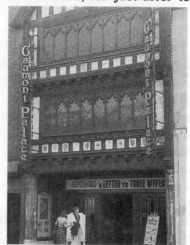

The Gaumont Palace entrance photographed in 1949, by which time the medieval theme used for its poster publicity had been dropped.

Mr Frank Crebo, Dad's foreman at Heaver's, came to tell him that for the first time in his life he was out of work. I remember just how embarrassed Mr Crebo was, for he and Dad had been friends for many years since they had worked together at Farr's before the Great War. It is no wonder that August 22nd, 1931 stands out in my memory — I ought to have been off to camp and that had been cancelled and now poor old Dad was without a job.

The following morning, Mum suggested that my father should accompany me, to cheer him up, so we went by train to Poole to visit my aunt, Dad's sister. She had a large family of eight, five daughters and three sons, all of whom except one were still living at home. I always enjoyed Poole as a boy — its bustling quay, nooks and crannys, the alleyways that enabled you to go from one side of the town to the other while hardly crossing a road. It was said that these had been made to enable men to avoid the attentions of the press gangs. Poole was a different world for me and how pleased I was when my aunt, on hearing that I was at a loose end, said that I could visit each day during the next week. My eldest male cousin made Dad laugh when he took us up to his bedroom to show off his handiwork. Alf had just had several months of unemployment and made use of the time to build a well constructed sideboard in his bedroom. Unfortunately, when the job was completed he found it was too large to go through the door! I don't know what happened to it — presumably there it stayed until the house was pulled down many years later, although I suppose once the roof was off the problem was solved. It was quite warm that day and for once we had no rain, so the whole family, with girl and boy friends a party of fifteen including Dad and me, went off to Branksome Chine. It was "to hell with the depression".

First thing on Monday, August 24th, I was off to Poole, little thinking just what a momentous day for the country was in store. Once again it rained, so after the midday meal I went with my three youngest cousins and two of their cousins to the Regent Cinema in High Street. It seemed a most sumptuous place, beautifully carpeted, and on that day showing Jean Harlow, known as the Blonde Bombshell, in Hell's Angels. During the interval I made acquaintance with a cinema organ for the first time and it left a lasting impression. The console appeared to rise from the depths, with the organist playing all the while, and for ten minutes we were treated to a first class recital.

Suddenly, in the middle of the feature film, the picture ceased and a hastily prepared hand written slide was flashed on the screen, informing us that the Labour Government had resigned. A national coalition was to be formed in view of the declining financial situation. The special edition of the *Bournemouth Echo* on sale as we left the cinema confirmed the news.

I thoroughly enjoyed that week at Poole and came to appreciate the beautiful scenery alongside the railway almost throughout the length of line from Salisbury. On the following Monday, I returned to work refreshed, which was just as well, for during my week away things had been happening. The new Gaumont Palace was due to be opened on Monday, September 7th and on Monday, August 24th when I had been at the Regent in Poole, the builders suddenly realised just how much sign-writing had to be carried out if the new theatre was to be issued with a safety certificate. The job was given to Mr Gething and he, with Fred Brooks (his other assistant), Tommy Haynes the sign-writer and Tommy's assistant, Hector MacDonald, had spent from daylight to dark trying to catch up with lost time. During that summer I had begun to despair of ever being trusted to produce a job on my own. Now, owing to the rush, I had just that chance. The former musical director of the Palace which had closed in May, thinking he had no chance of ever getting a similar job, had purchased a high class confectionery and tobacco business in the centre of Bournemouth. He had placed an order for about five gross of price tickets, which were ovals of black card and they were to be written in a particular shade of old gold with Trajan Roman figures. They only measured about one and three quarter inches high by one and a quarter inches across and so the prices were tiny, but I had always liked the smaller work.

Several times during that week, I had to go over to the new cinema with phone messages and the place seemed to be in chaos. There must have been hundreds of men working there. Scaffolding was still in place in the auditorium, electricians were shouting instructions to one another, oak panelling was still being fixed in the foyer, an army of painters could be seen, and I wondered just how the place could be ready for the grand opening on the following Monday. By the end of that week, all scaffolding had gone and two further armies of workers had appeared to lay carpets and install the seating. Work went on almost night and day over the weekend. On the morning of the seventh, I had to go with Mr Gething to paint some glass panels and write the instructions on the emergency fire alarms scattered through the building.

This was the first time that I realised the scale of the place. It was quite enormous. The entrance from The Canal was through The Halle of John Halle and the fifteenth century building looked very different from my previous visit, some ten years earlier, when it had been a china shop. Now it had resumed its original mantle of grandeur. The foyer with its oak panelling, the beautifully painted murals in the auditorium, the magnificent fire curtain (again hand painted), were all in keeping with the medieval entrance. I was amazed and more than impressed with the quality of the posters displayed. These had been produced by a London company and once again the fifteenth century theme was in evidence, as the film titles were written in Old English lettering, on a parchment type paper. The Gaumont Palace truly was unique. We finished our work on the fire alarms just before one o'clock, I remember the last one being inside the manager's office. Mr Victor Haydn, who had been appointed to run the new cinema (he had previously served as manager at the old Palace Theatre), was getting quite excited and seemed to be asking minute by minute how much longer we would be. As soon as the job was finished, he earned my everlasting gratitude when he presented me with two complimentary tickets for that night's performance. Mr Gething, as a contractor, had already been invited to the opening ceremony.

That evening, immediately after tea, I changed into my best suit and with a friend took my place in the back circle, the one and only time that I was able to sit in such an exalted position for many years. When we entered The Halle of John Halle, we were presented with a souvenir programme (printed in the fifteenth century theme) by one of the four diminutive page boys, each with carefully greased hair and a pair of white gloves tucked into a shoulder epaulette. The cinema also employed four tall, burly commissionaires, three of whom wore rows of medals (including the 1914 star) and some twenty usherettes. As my friend and I went across the foyer it seemed as if we would sink to our knees in the really beautiful carpet, which included the motif G.B. for Gaumont British in the design. On past the manager's office, where I had been working a few hours earlier, up the richly carpeted stairs and then we sighted the John Halle cafe to the left, where patrons were already being served in truly magnificent (for Salisbury) surroundings. We took a peep through the leaded glass of the doors, it was like looking at a film set. On up the stairs, to be met at the top by an usherette, who took our tickets and then with the help of a torch showed us to our seats. I mention this, because it was the first Salisbury cinema to have continuous performances. Both the Picture House and New Theatre still had matinées and nightly shows at 6.30pm and 8.45pm. Now the Gaumont was giving almost three hours of entertainment.

When the lights went up at the interval we had our first real look at the theatre. Words cannot describe the inspired work that we gazed on. The whole auditorium breathed a medieval air, not a discordant note to be seen. The architects had done a wonderful job and the directors of Gaumont British had produced a theatre of which Salisbury could be proud — it was the only one of its kind in the world. We sat back in the lovely armchair seating feeling like millionaires and enjoyed the antics of the Aldwych team — Tom Walls, Ralph Lynn, and Winifred Shotter — in the comedy *Chance of a Night Time.* Strangely, even the films seemed much better and in a different class to those shown at the other two cinemas, but I don't suppose they were.

On September 7th, 1981, I was a guest of honour at the theatre's Golden Jubilee celebration and assisted in the cutting of the birthday cake. I also attended the Diamond Jubilee celebrations in 1991. Where did those sixty years go?

The following day, work was back to normal. But not quite, as I was allowed to continue producing my black oval price tickets and from then on I was entrusted with a variety of simple posters and tickets. Life had become much more interesting. Now, as my friends and I walked around the city, I was able to point to something and say "I did that". I expect if I could see my early work again it would cause me to shudder.

That soccer season of 1931/32 ought to have been a successful one. The Salisbury and District League had announced a Boys' Section and we had entered. However, all our plans were kiboshed when the Rector of St Martin's, the Reverend W.N. Willson, decreed that only those attending Bible Class on a regular basis would be able to play in the football team. He held the whip hand, for we played at Shady Bower Field. Not only was it church property, we were also given the use rent free. A meeting was held, attended by the rector, who despite being almost accused of blackmailing, held firm and was adamant that the rule would be upheld. At the end of the meeting, four of our best players walked out saying they would never attend the class again and quickly became members of the Salisbury Boys' Club, run in conjunction with the YMCA. I had already been appointed captain and was left with the remnants of a team plus a number of fifteen-year-olds who had neither the weight nor skill to compete with players who were mostly two years older. It was a disastrous season. We won only one match and would have finished at the bottom of the league, had not

Salisbury City Football Club, 1931. The team included four ex-St Martin's players, Len Brown in goal, Johnny Hill, Charlie "Cheddar" Rattue and Fred Cook. Others I remember are Dewey, Burnham, Stoneham and Frampton. The chairman (seated centre) was Mr C. Kidd and the secretary (seated right) was Mr Gaisford.

St Francis, who were even worse than us, not played a well over age, unregistered player when they defeated us by four goals to three. We appealed and were given the two points which lifted us from the disgrace of holding up the table. Why did we appeal? We felt rather aggrieved because the over age player normally played for a Division One team and he had scored all our opponents' four goals.

Meanwhile, the coalition government which had been hastily thrown together under the leadership of Mr Ramsey MacDonald, gave the country shock after shock. We were virtually bankrupt, cuts had to be made, but no one guessed at the severity of these. Suddenly Britain abandoned the Gold Standard, the king-pin of our economy. Then the pay of police, civil servants and teachers was cut by ten per cent. Forces pay suffered a deduction of up to twenty five per cent and even the meagre dole money was reduced.

I was talking this period over with a friend, too young to remember those terrible times, and he remarked: "Arthur, if they tried it today, there'd be a revolution." It almost happened in 1931, for there were disturbances in major cities and a Naval riot took place at Ivergordon in Scotland. The depression which we had seen in the newsreels was now not only in America, it was here.

An election was called in October and all the Conservatives, Liberals and a few candidates from Labour stood under the banner of the National Party. The country, as so many times in history, woke up almost too late and began to pull together. Anyone speaking against the National Party was looked upon as a traitor. Lifelong political enemies in the city now shared the same platform and everyone was expecting great things from the new coalition.

On Polling Day, October 27th, a Tuesday, a large white screen was erected on the wall of the Wheatsheaf Inn. At about ten o'clock that evening, as results came in from constituencies around the country, the figures were projected on to the screen from a machine in the first floor window of the Southern Evening Echo on the other side of The Canal. When the first result came through, which showed a 30,000 majority for the National Candidate at Cheltenham, an enormous cheer went up from the crowd of possibly a thousand which had gathered. The cheer was repeated each time a victory for the coalition was flashed on the screen.

Most people were badly scared and nothing short of a miracle was expected of the new government. The next day, round about lunchtime, we learned that Major J. Despencer-Robertson had repeated his success of March and that the National Government had gained a Parliamentary majority of over five hundred.

Around this time, a start was made on the new Harnham Bridge which was to be built in line with Exeter Street. A house and laundry that had stood on the corner with St Nicholas Road had to be demolished. As soon as this was done, in the month or so before the bridge contractors were ready to commence operations, the site was filled with a "wall of death". This was a circular wall of timber, some thirty feet in height and diameter, with a ramp some six feet wide inside at the bottom. Riders on motor cycles started the machines, did a circuit or so on the flat, mounted the ramp and after a couple of circuits at a fairly sharp angle, opened their throttles and rode at full speed on the wall, riding almost horizontally. Then they did all sorts of stunts, diving from top to bottom as they went around, riding with hands off the machine, lighting a cigarette. Finally another rider would join the fun, the two criss-crossing at full speed. Suddenly, during the performance that I attended, the lights failed for about half a minute, but somehow the riders got down without harm. It was an exciting entertainment but did not attract many people on this tucked away site. I remember that when I went with several friends one Saturday evening I was sporting my first trilby hat, which my mother had persuaded me to buy. The other lads pulled my leg and I felt most self-conscious. Why, I don't know, because that trilby was only half the size of my scout hat. To return to the bridge, it was to be some two and a half years before it was completed. I believe the first contractors lost a great deal of money because the piles kept breaking as they hit a very hard level some fifteen feet below the river bed. The job was taken over by a second firm and, after several delays, New Bridge Road was completed and opened in the spring of 1934.

A feature of Salisbury in the Thirties was the printing of evening papers for the result of each horse race during the afternoons. Several newsvendors would dash out into the streets after the stop-press giving the results had been printed and put an end to the peace of our cathedral city. They were forced to shout for the competition was quite terrific. No less than four different titles had stop-press added at local works. The men (I can't remember any ladies) would run out at full speed calling "three o'clock result — *Southern Echo* (or the *News* or the *Star* or the *Standard*) — all the winners". How the service paid, heaven alone knows. However, all the noise finally broke the patience of the occupants of an office block in the city centre. A well known firm of solicitors and their accountant neighbours laid a complaint with the city police, who one afternoon pounced and arrested the offending newsvendors, who were charged under a local by-law. Dating from 1907, this read: "No person shall, for the purpose of hawking, selling, distributing or advertising any article, shout or use any bell, gong or other noisy instrument in any street or public place so as to cause annoyance to the inhabitants of the neighbourhood." When the case went to court, the complainants said that the shouting ruined their concentration, the defendants were found guilty and from then on, the city was somewhat quieter.

Although the new government entreated everyone to "Be British and Buy British", unemployment continued to rise sharply. By late October the queues of men lining up to sign on for the dole grew longer each week. At that time the Labour Exchange was in Catherine Street, some fifty yards from from the Ivy Street corner. Twice a day, in the morning and again in the afternoon, the column of workless stretched three or four men deep the length of the street, almost back to the Milford Street corner. An unemployed men's club was started in the Co-operative Hall in Winchester Street, loaned free of charge for the purpose. A representative of the Salisbury Unemployed Men's Association, Mr Barge, was elected to the City Council. Those who had a job, a regular job, thanked God. The unemployed just existed — the dole for a man was only eighteen shillings, and after six months appearance was ordered before a Means Test Tribunal, which had the authority to order the sale of anything owned which could be termed non-essential, such as a piano or a radio set. Those really were terrible times. In the manufacturing north, men spent years on the dole and even when war broke out in 1939 there were still many who had not worked since the late Twenties.

On a brighter note, there were still optimists ready to have a go. Crazy golf, which was played indoors and required little space, had swept the States in 1930. A Salisbury couple opened a small hall devoted to the new sport in Ashley Road, but their somewhat foolhardy venture in this out-of-the-way spot was short-lived and lasted only a few months. One business, commenced in 1931 against all the odds, was a high-class fish and chip shop. The owner, who had been head chef at the Cadena Cafe, started a new trend by announcing that everything was fried in pure lard. Even though times were hard and money was tight, his fish and chips, more expensive than those of his competitors, were an immediate success and the business prospered for many years.

A Portsmouth butcher started a greyhound racing track in Castle Road, then a breakaway group tried to launch a similar venture at West Harnham. Salisbury was not big enough for both, with the result that neither was successful and did not survive 1932.

In Rollestone Street, an entrepreneur did hit the right note with a billiard hall, having nine full size tables and a resident professional who, for a fee, would give lessons. However, though billiards was a game on the way out, snooker was rapidly taking its place and in consequence the venture was a success and ran for several years until the premises were purchased by the Wilts and Dorset Bus Company as part of a site for a bus station. Before the war, cinemas were closed on Sundays, so after attending evensong at church four of us would pool our resources, pay sixpence each and have a half-hour's snooker — a relaxation that left us feeling real men about town. The club had one table on the ground floor and four on each of the two upper storeys. The professional, Charlie Read, an excellent player, had a small cubby hole opposite the entrance doors where you paid your money. Charlie would tell you which table was free, sometimes a wait was necessary, then set the time clock corresponding to that table. You were always given three minutes to get to your appointed place before the overhead table lights came on. I remember when exhibition matches were played on a Wednesday evening between Willie Smith and Sidney Smith, who were in the top four national players, and Charlie Read. It was a splendid evening which left you with the feeling that your own efforts at the table were useless.

Late in 1931, work was halted on the Cunard liner 534 (later named the *Queen Mary*) which was being constructed on the Clyde. The decision meant that thousands lost their jobs and work was not resumed until early in 1933. The liner was eventually launched in October 1934.

Salisbury Market also felt the effects of the recession. On a Tuesday, a sheep attracted only one bid of two shillings and at this rock bottom price was knocked down to the well known greengrocer Mr Len Cannell. When asked by the local paper what he intended to do with the sheep, he replied that it would feed his greyhounds for a week!

Another event, which at that time created only a ripple of interest in this country, was Japan's invasion of Manchuria. We should have paid more attention because this was the beginning of the advancing Yellow Peril that Mr Spry, one of our masters at Bishop Wordsworth's School had talked of at great length. Japan was beginning to find her feet and the incursion into Manchuria against a very weak Chinese army was a rehearsal for what was to come ten years later. Yes, we should have paid more attention to those newsreel pictures.

Familiar sights in the city during the Twenties and Thirties were the billboard carts and sandwich board men. The carts were hand-carts with a billboard on each side. These measured ten feet by six feet eight inches and so took a sixteen-sheet poster. They were joined together at the apex and a triangular board was fixed at back and front to fill in the gaps. They could be hired from the Salisbury Bill-posting Company, one of Mr Albany Ward's many businesses, for one pound per day, excluding the cost of posters and billposting. Men to push the contraptions around the city were easily obtained from the Labour Exchange — their rate of remuneration being five shillings for the day. The same rate was paid to those who carried sandwich boards measuring some three feet six inches by two feet six inches. The men were not expected to keep on the move all the time and although pushing the carts was heavier work, at least the shafts did supply a seat in between moves of perhaps a hundred yards at the stretch. Men on the dole were offered this work and provided they were not sick, had to accept or risk the possibility of a cut in dole money. Doubtless both the carts and the sandwich boards offered a cheap form of publicity.

For some two weeks or so, at Christmas 1931, a fair made its appearance, at, of all places, the Market House. There was no "fair atmosphere" in this unlikely venue and the experiment was never repeated. I remember that on the afternoon of Boxing Day, the city team defeated a strong Metropolitan Police XI at Victoria Park, a friendly fixture which they had been expected to lose. Two of the city's goals were scored by a newcomer, Cyril Smith, who usually played in the local league for St Edmunds.

Chapter Six 1932
Finding my feet

On a cold and very frosty night in January 1932, a fire broke out at the rear of Woodrows, the Castle Street ironmongers. The premises ran right back to the Mill Stream of the River Avon and the shop premises fronted the street, while behind were a myriad of stores and workshops, most of them dating back many a long year — they might be described as a tinderbox. The only entrances to this part of the premises were via a long yard at the side of the shop in Castle Street and a wooden footbridge across the river leading from a footpath which ran from the Town Mill. At the time, Salisbury Volunteer Fire Brigade was still in operation and that night they did a wonderful job in controlling a blaze in a pretty inaccessible spot, something which they did quite often that year.

The thing that made this night memorable was that one of their members almost lost his life. This particular chap was a well known character who, living life to the full, could usually be found at one or other of the city hostelries. That night, he had been inbibing in his usual way and was not too quick off the mark when the alarm went. He turned up rather late and ran up the riverside path, across the tiny footbridge which was railed by a single bar on either side, lost his footing and went into the fast flowing stream below. As this happened in January, the river was quite high and as the poor chap was wearing his brass helmet, for a while things did not look too good for him. However, thanks to his colleagues he was pulled out, no doubt having sobered very, very quickly.

We now began to have social evenings for those attending the Bible Classes. Perhaps our elders felt that now at the ages of sixteen and seventeen it was safe for these to be mixed functions. Most of the time was taken up with various games — it was all very innocent. One evening, I spotted a new girl, who had come from her home some ten miles away to work in the city. At first, I just admired from afar, but after a week or two, plucked up sufficient courage to ask if she would like to go to the pictures and was quite surprised when she said "Yes". I met her at about seven o'clock on a Tuesday evening and we went surruptitiously via the back streets to the Catherine Street entrance of the Gaumont.

It cost me one shilling and tenpence for two centre stall seats and the film was hardly a romantic choice. Called *The Big House,* it featured Wallace Beery and was the story of an American prison riot. We came out, I took E--- home and as I wished her goodnight said I hoped to see her after Bible Class on Sunday. I was seventeen, she a few months younger. We used to meet once or twice a week after that. It was about three months before word got back to my family and another three before we visited our respective homes. Although we held hands as we wandered along on walks around the city outskirts, four months were to pass before our first kiss. This harmless romance lasted about eight months by which time I was missing the companionship of my friends and was beginning to be scared as the young lady started to say "When we are married". So on another Tuesday, in October, I made my excuses and said goodbye.

There had been a Naval riot in the previous September, now there was a prison riot at Dartmoor. We were shocked when listening to the nine o'clock news on a Sunday evening to hear of the outbreak of violence that morning when almost a hundred convicts and warders had been injured. We were told how Marines had been rushed by coach to the prison, which was surrounded by machine guns to deter any escape attempts. Dad said he never thought such a thing could ever happen in England.

On a Tuesday, just prior to Easter 1932, the whole of Ewens' staff were gathered on the pavement in Winchester Street, opposite where I was working. We soon learnt that the old-established motor wholesalers had "gone bust".

The firm, founded by Benjamin Ewen (a jobmaster — one who hired out horses and carriages), had appeared to be a thriving concern and no doubt the problem was the same "cash-flow" of which so much has been heard in recent years. The chief salesman, Mr Sidney Chalk, had started Radio Services in a shop belonging to

Ewens. This had been run by his brother, Wilfred. Now the business moved to much larger premises on the other side of the street and Sidney took charge. Ewens were closed for a few weeks, then re-opened, under the leadership of a lady (who later became Mrs. Townsend) and through her guidance was a prosperous concern for the next forty five years.

That year, Easter Sunday was very early, March 27th. In fact it has only been earlier five times in this century. As usual, I went to early service on Good Friday and came away from church breathing a sigh of relief that the rest of the day was mine. Hardly the right attitude, but after all I was only seventeen. That evening Salisbury saw an innovation, a special show at the Gaumont Palace. It was the first time a local cinema had opened on Good Friday. The management had asked for special permission from the Watch Committee and consent was given subject to a suitable programme for the special day, so the film shown, *Smilin' Through,* was a bit of a weepie which featured Norma Shearer.

Crowds queued to pack a cinema that after the initial good business had begun to feel the cold wind of recession, resulting in a reduction of price for the front stalls from ninepence to sixpence. That evening we had marvellous value for our tanners, because during an extended interval we were entertained by the manager's wife, Mrs Haydn, who had been a concert violinist. Her rendering of *The Flight of the Bumblebee* really brought the house down.

I had to work on Saturday morning, as we had a shipping order for Playfairs, the footwear retailers who had a small shop in Fisherton Street. We had done a set of four price cards for the local shop, these were in spring colours, green on a bright yellow card. They had caught the area manager's eye and he placed an order for a set for each of his twenty four shops.

Immediately after lunch, we were off to play football against Wilton Boys. It was pouring with rain and we had to change in their club room in a lane off North Street, then, in football kit, walk to the ground near the Wilton Park Sawmills in South Street, a distance of at least half a mile. Wilton believed in wearing down the visiting team before the match and when we arrived we found the pitch, which adjoined the River Nadder, to be a real mudpatch.

I am not putting that forward as an excuse for our 6-2 defeat, for Wilton were a good side.

Sunday was another wet day but this did not make any difference to the church attendance which was expected of me. I went at 7am, 11.30am, 2.30pm and 6.30pm. I think parents would have a problem to get their seventeen-year-old children to attend four times these days, but it didn't hurt us.

On Monday, the rain ceased and we had a friendly match at Shady Bower, which was a quagmire both in the goal areas and the centre circle. During the match, I was severely kicked on the shin and finished with a bad limp but this did not stop me from going out in the evening for I had a date with a young lady. After meeting E--- off the bus we went to the Picture House to see Erich Remarque's film *All Quiet on the Western Front,* which showed trench warfare as seen through German eyes. I must have been naive to take her to such a film for after watching about fifteen minutes of the picture, which had many scenes of slaughter, E--- said that she didn't feel too well, so out we went. I took her home and then went back to see the end of the film. (I must have been callous as well as naive.)

The New Theatre in Castle Street, which had shown "talkies" for about two years, was suffering from the competition of the Gaumont Palace. It was owned by Gaumont British (as was the Picture House) and the management decided to close it at the end of April. Just prior to that date, a film to which we had looked forward for weeks was shown, it starred the whole of the Arsenal team, our heroes throughout the Thirties. In the event, the film *The Great Game* was a bit of a let down — I've never yet seen soccer well portrayed in any film or television play.

The last match of that season was a friendly played against St Thomas' Old Boys on a very wet evening at Shady Bower. The pitch, which was heavier than I had ever known it, became worse as the game progressed. The ball was eventually like a lump of lead. It was a hard fought match (we lost 2-1) and just before the final whistle one of the opposing forwards shot just as I went in to tackle. I took the drive bang in the face and my nose began to stream blood. Within a short time it was swelling and took a week or so to return, as I thought, to normal. One day, my mother said:

"What's the matter with your nose — it's crooked," and I was sent off to the doctor. His diagnosis was that I must have broken it, so I was dispatched to the Infirmary, where a specialist said I should go in to stay. He explained that the bone would have to be broken again and reset, or I would suffer illness as I became older. I went home, thought about it, chickened out, nothing was ever done and to date (I'm nearly seventy seven) no problems.

Radio had brought a new dimension, all the big sporting events were now eagerly awaited for we could listen to live commentaries. The Cup Final that year was between Arsenal and Newcastle. The former, champions of Division I the previous year, had finished the season as runners-up while the latter were way down in mid-table. Consequently Arsenal were hot favourites but Newcastle won by two goals to one. The winning goal came from a centre from the right and Arsenal protested vigorously that the ball had gone out of play before the final pass was made. The radio commentator agreed but the referee was adamant and allowed the goal to stand. Thanks to modern science, the Sunday newspapers were able to print pictures with suitably enlarged close-ups showing that the ball really had been over the byline and they felt the Football Association should order the game to be replayed. Fuel was added to the flames when the cinemas showed newsreels on the Monday proving the referee's error. We argued for days but the result stood. One memory I have from that newsreel is of the Newcastle wing half, the first player to make a name for himself by being able to take a throw-in and reach the goal area. This feat is now quite commonplace, but Sam Weaver showed back in 1932 how it could be done.

At the beginning of the summer term, my eldest sister started teaching at the Highbury Avenue Junior Council School and was to stay there for the next fourteen years. She had previously spent three years at All Saints School at Edmonton and just after starting her new job she asked if I could design a new school badge. I submitted two designs and one of these, approved by the headmistress, was used for the next thirty years. It was a simple monogram of JC in a lozenge of rather Edwardian design. I was quite proud to have done this job and used to look out for those wearing the green cap with a creamy yellow badge.

My aunt had retired the previous year and she went one afternoon with my mother to view their parents' grave in the London Road cemetery. On their return home they decided that something must be done about the memorial stone which, placed as it was beneath trees, had become a lovely shade of pale green. A local mason was asked to give an estimate for renovation, to clean the stone and repaint the incised lettering. The cost shocked my aunt, who then asked me if I would do the job for fifteen shillings, half the mason's estimate. I went along and viewed the work and readily agreed. Fifteen shillings was a fortune to me, it was more than my take-home pay for a week. So on a Saturday afternoon, armed with a pair of shears and a piece of bath stone I started the task. After about three hours and much rubbing with the bath stone and constant supplies of clean water, the memorial was bright and shining. Next I trimmed the grass, and the following week spent some four hours lying on my stomach filling in the lettering with a specially prepared black paint that was quickly absorbed into the stone. Fifty years later I found that the black was still as good as the day the job was done and the fungicide with which I had painted the stone had to a large extent stopped it from becoming green. When I was paid my fifteen shillings I felt rich but I've often wondered how I looked lying on my stomach in the cemetery.

As part of the growing up process some youngsters develop acne, some develop boils. I developed styes. Fortunately, in my case the problem was shortlived, but I shall never forget the Whitsun weekend of 1932. I had been looking forward to the break, but had to spend the whole two and a half days indoors as both eyes were almost completely gummed up and it was painful. My father laughed at the pitiful sight and told me not to worry, it was all part of the transition from boyhood to manhood. The phase lasted, in all, about three weeks, although I was devoid of eyelashes for many months.

An innovation at this time was the arrival on the market of Brylcreem. Within a short time, we had all become "Brylcreem Boys". Gone was the greasy solid brilliantine, now, although it was much more expensive, the new cream swept away almost all opposition. Mothers still groused about dirty pillows but no-one thought of appearing in public without a daily application of the new wonder hair dressing. The barbers were doing well because most males under thirty went for a cut at fortnightly intervals at a cost of sixpence a time.

A craze from America swept the country that summer. It was simple, it was inexpensive and most people tried the new fad. It was the Yo-Yo. The *Bristol Evening World* stole a march on its rivals by the organisation of a big money prize contest with local heats and a grand final in Bristol. The really clever exponents of Yo-Yo were not content to just jig the thing up and down, they could perform a variety of tricks — one of these I remember was "walking the dog". This meant throwing the Yo-Yo so that it ran on the ground away from you. When it reached the end of the string, you gave it a sharp tug, it wound itself back to the hand and the trick was repeated.

Talking about the *Bristol Evening World* reminds me of two stories of around 1932, when the ace reporter who was trying to get a foothold in Salisbury really excelled himself. The stop-press was printed at a Bedwin Street Printers and the reporter used the premises as his HQ. One afternoon he was short of a sensational story, essential if papers were to be sold, so he chased around to drum something up. Demolition men were pulling down old houses in an Endless Street Court and our ace reporter asked them if they had found anything. "Yes, a skeleton hanging from roof timbers," was the reply. The paper came out, with placards announcing "Skeleton found hanging in Salisbury roof". The story was well padded, no untruths, "the coroner will be informed" etc, but our reporter omitted to say that the hanging skeleton of indeterminate age was that of a cat!

On another occasion a real faux pas was made at the Bristol headquarters of the paper. Each evening a Salisbury page was included and, as an insurance against insufficient copy, several photos of city landmarks were kept in reserve to fill any blank spaces. One evening a photo was needed and an excellent view of Fisherton Clock Tower appeared. Underneath was the caption "The Clock Tower in Fisherton Street, Salisbury, which chimes the passing hours above the busy city". Our ace reporter was never allowed to forget this almighty clanger (sorry), the clock has always been silent, for the simple reason that it does not possess the necessary mechanism to enable it to strike or chime.

Derby Day 1932 turned out to be a wonderful day for me. At about midday, I was asked to buy a ticket in the Crown Chambers' lottery and spent my last sixpence, not liking to say no to the request. Just before one o'clock, Mr Gething's friend who sold me the ticket rang to tell me that I had drawn a horse, April the Fifth, owned by Mr Tom Walls (the actor and film star). I went home with the news. I'd never heard of the horse, but found out that the possible starting price was a hundred to six, borrowed a shilling from my sister and backed it, as did my mother and aunt. It was an inspired action, for it won. At about four-thirty I was paid the sweepstake prize of two whole pounds. The following day, after receiving the winnings from my bet, I took myself off to Dad's friend Mr E.P. Adlam (he later became mayor) who had an outfitters shop on the corner of Milford Street with Brown Street and with my two pounds, sixteen shillings was able to purchase a tweed sports coat, a decent pair of flannels and two shirts. That two pounds, sixteen shillings was probably worth a hundred pounds in 1991 currency.

Thus it was that I was so well dressed at that time, for a week or so later my new navy blue suit, which had been made to measure by Montague Burton (the Tailor of Taste), arrived in good time for my sister's wedding on Wednesday, June 29th. My father, however, cut it fine, for on the morning of the big day he had to visit the dentist to take delivery of his first dental plates. These were fitted only about two hours prior to his walking up the aisle to give his daughter away. It was a beautiful day and by three o'clock the proceedings were over and with two of my female cousins who were all arrayed in their finery, I walked to Old Sarum. It seemed strange to be free on a normal working day but I remember that I had already worked eight hours extra time in order to have that day off.

The following day, Thursday, Dad came home from work to say that once again he had been stood off. After losing his job the previous August, he had some four or five weeks on the dole, was re-employed for six weeks or so, and from November through to March was again idle. After four and a half months without

*All dressed up and nowhere to go — a favourite
expression of the author's father. The photo, of the
author, his mother, father and younger sister Margaret
(then eight), was taken on the day of his sister Gladys's
wedding. The author and his father had been suited by
Montague Burton "the tailor of taste". The cost of each
three-piece suit (made to measure) was £2 7s 6d.*

work. Just as both he and the whole family were beginning to be worried about a possible appearance before a Means Test Tribunal, he was able to resume work at Heavers of Durrington. This spell lasted from March to the end of June. During those months of unemployment, Dad was never idle, he made all sorts of items from scrap wood including a chest of drawers, the timber for which came from Tate & Lyle sugar boxes. Anyone seeing the finished job would never have guessed the material's origin, the drawers were beautifully dovetailed and the whole had a lovely finish. I think Dad had found the answer to enforced unemployment — creating things was far better than hanging around street corners as so many of his contemporaries were quite content to do. Fortunately this proved to be his last spell on the dole, for in August Mr Bob Inglefield, the foreman at The Friary works of Edwards Brothers, came to see Dad and asked if he would like a job as general handyman at a wage far below that which he had received at Heavers. My father was only too pleased to accept and stayed with Edwards until his enforced retirement through ill-health in 1946. I've often thought of the early days when I used to chase off every night to meet my father. At that time coach-building was one of the elite trades, yet only some fourteen years later it was dying due to mass production. I think its demise almost broke Dad's heart.

The recession brought an end to an old-established Salisbury family business when Wiltons on The Canal almost went into liquidation. They were not only wholesale and retail ironmongers, silversmiths, heating engineers, plumbers and general smiths but had departments for leather goods and general gifts. Almost sixty people were employed there. Fortunately, one of the main creditors purchased the goodwill and moved the business to the recently vacated New Theatre cinema in Castle Street where it continued for another forty years. Wiltons' palatial premises, with its extensive yard at the rear, were acquired by The Salisbury Electric Light and Supply Company, who moved from their tiny showrooms in the Cheese Market. They installed one of the first plate glass windows, using two concave sections which eliminated reflection. Meanwhile, Mr Wilton carried on the sports shop, at the corner of The Canal and Queen Street. It had been saved from the debacle and he commenced serving in the shop, something which he had never done before. He eventually sold the business to a Mr Kidwell in the mid-Thirties. Mr Wilton, a kindly man, had given so much to the city especially the Chamber of Commerce, having been its President and Treasurer and in his adversity received the sympathy of all who knew him.

On August Monday, the Salisbury Motor Cycle Club, who normally promoted grass track meetings, put on something very different — T.T. type races at Wilbury Park, some ten miles from the city, the home of Major J. Despencer Robertson, MP. I suppose it was exciting, but unless you were near the finish you had no idea of what was going on or who was winning. Taking part were two members who had raced in the T.T. races on the Isle of Man, Paddy Cash and Bill Wareham, but as a spectator I was more than disappointed. E--- and I had arranged to take the same week for our holidays and went for cycle rides around Salisbury, with the exception of one day when we went by coach excursion to Bournemouth and it rained almost throughout the day.

We had excitement in September — two quite severe fires. The first occurred during the early hours of one morning when I was awakened by a tremendous noise of crackling and my bedroom itself seemed to be on fire. I got up, looked out of the window and huge flames could be seen above the roof of Gibbs, Mew and Co's Gigant Street brewery, only about a hundred yards away. By this time, my father was also awake and joined me by the window. It looked as if the building must be doomed. We dressed quickly and arrived in Gigant Street at almost the same time as the Brigade, who fortunately were able to get the fire under control in less than an hour. The blaze had appeared far worse than it really was, as it started near the base of the chimney, which must have been some sixty feet high and provided the fire with a draught so that the flames had the appearance of a blow torch on top of the stack. There was an amusing sequel. When Dad and I got home, the rest of the family were enjoying a cup of tea in true British fashion. We joined them and Mum suddenly said to me: "What's up with your waistcoat?" In my haste to get to the fire I had put the thing on inside out.

Shortly after the Gibbs Mew blaze, Salisbury suffered another serious fire — this time in the early hours of a Tuesday, when Mitre House went up in flames. The building, situated at the corner of New Street and High Street, is famed as the house where every new Bishop of Salisbury enrobes prior to his consecration in the nearby Cathedral. I knew nothing of the fire until reaching work in the morning and it was not long after that we received a visit from a man in a very great hurry. He was the proprietor of the high-class Ladies' hairdressing establishment which occupied Mitre House. Considering his ordeal of the night before, he was quite composed, for he with his wife and young children had only just escaped from their flat above the shop, by climbing through a trap-door on to the roof and from there to the roof next door. The fire had left the place a blackened shell and he now required a large poster in double-quick time announcing that after necessary rebuilding and repairs the business would be re-opened as quickly as possible. I recollect that he had been insured with the Phoenix Insurance Company, so at the top of the poster he wanted a representation of the fabled bird, which also rose from the ashes.

Owing to the difficulties of the previous season, it was decided to disband the St Martin's Boys' Football Team and I started the new season with St Mark's, for whom I played three games. A new curate then arrived at the church and wanted to resurrect the soccer team. He persuaded the rector to somewhat modify his demand of the year before, that all players must be regular attendants at the Sunday Bible Class. As it was too late to enter the Salisbury and District League, the reformed team had to fall back on friendly matches. But we were no longer short of players, the problem was who to leave out. For a time the Bible Class was extremely well attended, but by the end of a successful season, which promised well for the future, no more than fifty per cent of the regular side were to be seen on Sundays.

Workwise, I had gained a great deal of confidence in the last twelve months and was now entrusted with many jobs, one of which I did weekly for almost twenty years. This was the Gaumont Palace time sheets, small cards, measuring seven inches in width by ten inches high and carrying the daily programme. When one allowed space at the top for the heading, "Gaumont Palace — Today's Programme", you were left with about six inches to write the names and times of each film. This often ran to fifteen items and The King was always added at the foot, so the lettering was only one third of an inch in height. I produced some two thousand of these cards (two per week), so although it is over forty years since I last wrote them, I could even now almost do the job blindfold. The cost of these cards at the theatre's opening in 1931 was three shillings and sixpence and remained at that figure for over ten years. This was for about an hour's work and included visiting the Gaumont at 10am on Saturdays, when local suppliers had to line up outside the manager's office for payment.

During that year, the national papers had plenty to report. For weeks we were entertained by the antics of the Rector of Stifkey, a village in Norfolk. He was brought before a Consistory Court, charged with immoral behaviour. The "Sundays" especially had a field day, as evidence was brought that the sixty-year-old clergyman was only at his church to take the Sunday services and the rest of his time was spent at his "love-nest" in London, which was frequented by prostitutes. While the hearing was continuing, he returned to his church on one Sunday and struggled with the locum-tenens who was conducting the service. After the lengthy hearing, the case was found to be proved and he was ordered to be defrocked. Utterly disgraced, he spent the next five years appearing in side shows, among other places at Blackpool, and in 1937 as he entered a cage, was mauled by a lion and killed.

After many years of negotiation, the various factions of the Methodist Church at last united, although the five Salisbury churches (two Wesleyan, two Primitive and one United Methodist) continued over many years. Today, only one remains.

To celebrate the first anniversary of the opening of the Gaumont Palace, a silver christening cup was to be given to the first baby born in Salisbury on September 7th. Plans had to be quickly altered when the wife of Mr Martin Wilce, a proof reader employed by Salisbury Press, gave birth to twins and the embarrassed father had to make a stage appearance to receive not one, but two cups.

In November of 1932 there was trouble at mill, when cotton workers were asked to accept a pay cut, resulting in a week-long strike. The workers then found they had no alternative but to return to their jobs.

The month also saw the beginning of the Hunger Marches to London. The economic situation had deteriorated and pitched battles were reported in London streets. Some papers believed that these were Communist inspired and that the National Unemployed Workers' Movement was being funded by the Russian Government.

The year ended, however, on a peaceful note, when on Christmas Day, His Majesty King George V spoke to the nation in the first of his Christmas broadcasts.

Chapter Seven 1933
Adolf casts his shadow

Looking back after almost sixty years, it seems impossible that we could ever get so het up over cricket. In early 1933, the Test Matches were being played in Australia and in an effort to regain the Ashes, a plan was hatched by the English captain, D.R. Jardine, to employ his fast bowlers (he had a squad of four) to use deliveries which were quickly dubbed "bodyline". In the matches played in England in 1930, the Australian batsman Bradman, well supported by several other excellent players, had run up huge scores. They all crouched in such a way that the poor bowlers could never see the wicket and were wonderful exponents of the art of batting. Jardine's plan was to bowl just outside the leg stump and one of his bowlers, Larwood, was so fast (he was timed at 95 miles per hour) that the Australian batsmen had to move across the wicket and ended up playing ineffectual shots that gave catches to the six fielders gathered in an arc on the leg side.

Suddenly the Australians realised that even with Don Bradman they could be beaten. Several of their players were struck with the ball and their captain, Woodfull, complained "Its not cricket". They overlooked the batting of one of their own team, Stan McCabe, who continued to get runs because he was so nimble on his feet. As England were winning the third test, all hell was let loose. The Aussies threatened to cancel the fourth and fifth matches and the MCC said they would bring the team home.

In this country, bodyline became the one topic of conversation, the feeling being that the Australians were just bad losers. The games were brought to us by means of radio — we were never more than five minutes late with the score. Each morning from six a.m. we tuned into Radio Normandy, a French station that broadcast commercially sponsored programmes beamed at this country. In between the lengthy advertisements, cables from the Australian test grounds were read, giving the up-to-date scores and details. It was to us at that time quite amazing that we knew within a few minutes what was happening on the other side of the world.

Fortunately tempers cooled, both here and in Australia and the tour was completed, but the MCC never forgave Jardine or his henchmen Larwood and Voce. Harold Larwood must have been a very brave man, for a few years later, he upped sticks and emigrated to the land where he had been so reviled.

In January 1933, Aubrey Searle, caretaker of St Martin's Men's Club, suggested that as I was now 18 I might like to join. I needed no second bidding and began to learn how to play billiards and snooker properly. The club had two full size tables, one was excellent, the other very slow, with cushions that had lost much of their elasticity. The good table was used for league matches against other clubs and unless you were in the club by 6.30 p.m. it was quite impossible to get a game on it as the bookings board was always full of the chalked initials of those staking their claim. As a result, the poor table was usually used by younger and inexperienced players.

At that time St Martin's ran two sides of six in the billiards league. A snooker league had not yet been formed. The club had a number of players who were of a high standard and although billiards was still played, they spent most evenings on the new love of snooker. A game between the top exponents playing a foursome, would sometimes take an hour, each shot being played, after great discussion, as though the fate of the world depended on it. I spent many an evening watching them and listening to the constant arguments.

A month or so after I became a member, I introduced two friends; they in their turn brought others and within six months there were possibly twenty of my age group. The older hands were pleased to see us as there had been a dearth of new members for several years.

St Martin's was also noted for its table tennis prowess, although it must be said that in those days the game was more reminiscent of its original name "ping-pong". The players were never more than two feet from the table and apart from a few coming into the city, had no idea how far behind Salisbury Table Tennis lagged. Everyone had a rude awakening when an exhibition match was played at our club on a Saturday evening by four Middlesex county players, three of whom were internationals. It was a revelation — they were so much faster. Their normal stance at the beginning of a point was anything from two to five feet from the table, they could retrieve a ball some ten feet back and their mastery of spin when serving left us somewhat breathless.

At last it was time for one of their number to play the Salisbury champion, Bill Gulliver, who up to then we had thought was first class. I was talking to the exhibition organiser when the Middlesex opponent came up and asked "What shall we do, make it a game or just an exhibition". He was told to make a game of it. It was slaughter, it was embarrassing. Our champion lost by 21-1. That evening was a turning point for local table tennis and standards rapidly improved. Players today can watch the best in the world by means of television. They can video games in order to keep looking and see how it should be done. I suppose the same applies to snooker, for here again the local standard is very different to the game played nearly sixty years ago.

1933 saw the first Salisbury Snooker Championship and as the final was between two St Martin's players it was decided that the match should be played at our club. Harry Harold, who must have been around the forty mark, was favourite to beat his younger opponent Bruce Naish. He was a self employed carpenter and undertaker while Bruce was in charge of a builder's office. The first two games went easily to Harry, but then Bruce made a fightback and levelled the scores. In the final game it was best of five. Harry built up a useful lead, which Bruce wiped out before going ahead by some twenty points with only four balls, brown, blue, pink and black, left on the table, a total of twenty two. Bruce was still in play and only wanted brown to win. I remember vividly his opponent remarking in a loud voice as he rubbed his arm: "Been on a heavy job today, sawing most of the time, no good for this game." Whether this put Bruce right off his stroke I don't know, but in any case he missed a simple pot. Harry then played four first-class shots, potting brown, blue, pink and black to win the championship. No-one heard any more about the heavy sawing.

A week or so later we had a celebration dinner, where a splendid array of trophies was on show. The club had made almost a clean sweep, with the individual local champions for snooker and table tennis and team championships in the table tennis league divisions one, two and three. The cost for the meal was only one shilling and sixpence per head, but I think one or two of the more affluent members must have subsidised the event.

I wrote in a previous chapter that the Arsenal soccer team were our heroes. Not only were they wonderful players, the team also possessed a reputation for fair play second to none. In the third round of the FA Cup in 1932/3 they were drawn against lowly Walsall, then a struggling Third Division North side. Although the game was to be played at Walsall, Arsenal were a certainty to win. That afternoon, we had a game against Woodford United and went to the match by Rowlands' fourteen-seater Rolls-Royce coach. This must have been the one and only Rolls-Royce used for this purpose. It was a real oldie and though Rowlands had just plonked the coach body on to an extremely long car chassis, it was a most comfortable ride. We had an excellent match, being strengthened by the presence of George Handford, a locally well known left half, and he set us on our way by floating over two crosses which I was fortunate enough to net with my head. After two minutes we were two up and went on to win by four goals to one.

We returned on the coach to Blue Boar Row where newsvendors were shouting "Full-time Results". We bought some papers and were astounded, shocked and concussed to read Walsall two, Arsenal nil. It was the cup upset of all time. True, owing to an outbreak of 'flu, Arsenal fielded five reserves, but how could they ever lose? The discussion went on for days. The second Walsall goal came as the result of a penalty awarded for a blatant trip by an Arsenal reserve full back. This was looked on by the club's directors as really letting down the Arsenal image and the player was immediately put on the transfer list. What a pity that some modern day directors don't follow this example of sportsmanship.

Just after this, the shadow of Hitler began to fall across our world. He ruined the Thirties with his rantings and ravings, which came to us via radio and newsreels. At the end of January, when we were arguing about "bodyline", he became German Chancellor

Cycling days: The author with his sister Margaret (on saddle) and cousin Dorothy.

St Martin's Boys Football Club 1933. Back row: the Reverend F.C. Colyer, N. Day (linesman), H. Uphill, W. Heather, T. Burden, A. Stone, A. Bennett, A. Harding, and A. Searle (coach).
Front row: D. Cooper, R. Roper, L. Pinner, A. Maidment (captain), and C. Adlam.

and from then on, almost every month prior to the outbreak of war in 1939, we read of another outrage, another demand; of the unprecedented growth of Nazi forces and the ill treatment of Jews, but few wanted to listen. The motto was "forget it and it will go away". Within a month of Hitler taking office the Reichstag went up in flames, and for weeks we saw pictures of a poor, mentally retarded Dutchman, Van Der Leibbe, who was charged with arson and later executed. In April came the first pictures of violence against the Jews, in June all opposition parties were abolished, and from then on Germany was a virtual dictatorship.

While all these things were happening, Britain just carried on as normally as possible with three million people unemployed. At least 1933 was a wonderful summer weatherwise, and with my friends I made the most of it. Once again, St Martin's had no cricket team, so I had to find other pursuits and turned again to cycling. In earlier years I had explored South Wiltshire, now a hundred miles in a day was a doddle. A friend and I spent every weekend off on a jaunt, dressed for the occasion in cycling shorts and open-necked shirts, with rolled oilskins strapped to the top of carrier bags attached to the saddles of our bikes.

At this time my take-home pay was eighteen shillings and tenpence, so I had little pocket money. We used to take our food for the day and seldom spent money while on our trips. On many weekday mornings during that lovely summer we would go off at about six thirty and cycle twenty miles or so before going home for a quick breakfast and then work. In the evenings we would be off again, as a result our runs at the weekend were no problem — we possibly went on pedalling away in our sleep.

If you draw a circle around Salisbury with a radius equivalent to forty-five miles, you will see just what wonderful trips we enjoyed. The coast was well within reach, as were Swindon, Bath, Dorchester, Bournemouth, Poole, Christchurch, Portsmouth, Petersfield, Basingstoke and Newbury. That year rain was seldom a problem, although I do remember what a horrible trip we had when caught in a heavy storm at Alton. We waited for it to stop, decided that it wouldn't, and continued via Basingstoke and Andover — cycling the last fifteen miles in the dark without lights. Fortunately we did not meet with the law. I was met by an irate father who knew I had not taken my lamp and Mum was sure that an accident must have happened. They were wonderful days and we got fitter all the time.

Each Saturday afternoon I went up to Harnwood Hospital on the outskirts of Salisbury to see a friend who was suffering from tuberculosis, which had been diagnosed the previous September. N had had stomach pains and was rushed to the Infirmary, where it was found he had TB of the intestinal tract. He remained in that hospital for about a couple of months before returning home but then had to be admitted to Harnwood, of which it was said "nobody ever comes out of there alive".

The first time I went to visit N, I was shocked by the look of the patients — young men, many little older than me but with the gaunt faces of old men. It brought home to me just how important is health, without it we have nothing. After several weeks in the ward, N was moved to a one-bed chalet in the beautiful grounds, overlooking the city and with an unsurpassed view of the Cathedral. Harnwood had been the home of Bishop Wordsworth, founder of my old school. It was then purchased by the local Member of Parliament, Mr Geoffrey Locker-Lampson, prior to being bought for use as a hospital. It was only one of many in Wiltshire catering for those afflicted with the deadly disease, which was such a scourge before the discovery of streptomycin and the early diagnosis by mass x-ray. N was lucky, for after several months of living in the healthy atmosphere of that chalet he was able to return home, and following a long period of recuperation resumed work. I saw him again in 1990, when almost sixty years after being virtually written off he looked in the best of health.

In late summer, Salisbury began to wonder if Britain was to follow Germany's example when Sir Oswald Mosley's Blackshirts took over the city centre. The movement seemed to be gaining support in some of the larger centres of population and the reports of violence which we read in the papers and saw in the newsreels were not confidence inspiring. When Sir Oswald came to address a meeting at the Victoria Hall, his henchmen were dressed in black shirts, black trousers and wide leather belts, and their hair was almost cropped. The streets rang to their cries of "Mosley speaks. Three p.m. Victoria Hall. Read The Blackshirt". All the while they were thrusting the magazine in front of every passer-by, most of whom were so frightened that they meekly handed over the price of threepence and were glad to make their escape. A friend of mine who was attending Bishop Wordsworth's School went to the meeting with several of his colleagues, one of whom had the temerity to ask questions during question time. He was forcibly ejected by Sir Oswald's thugs and my friend admits that he was scared to death. However, the attempt by the leader of the British Union of Facists to spread the doctrine in South Wiltshire was a non-starter.

During that summer we were quite busy at work producing posters for a mobile poster vehicle. At the end of 1932, Mr Fred Hancock, the proprietor of the Lithanode Battery Service in Fisherton Street, had been declared bankrupt. With the help of friends his wife had managed to keep the business running through 1931, while he too was in hospital with TB, but unfortunately it fell victim to the recession. He bought a car that was just post-war, with a folding hood. This was fitted with an advertising board on either side and one at the back. The poster space was let by the day and as a result it provided quite a lot of work for us. One of the advantages of this project against the hand-carts was the fact that the car could be driven to events attracting large crowds. I remember that Style and Gerrish's summer sale was advertised in this way at Salisbury Racecourse in July.

My friend and I decided to extend the area of our cycling over the August Bank Holiday (it was then the first weekend in that month) to visit my uncle in Tottenham, London, a ride of ninety three miles in each direction. How were we to know that it was to be the hottest Bank Holiday of the century? We started away at seven o'clock on Sunday morning and made our way via the Bourne Valley to Cholderton, then on to Andover and to Basingstoke, where we stopped for a cup of tea at a transport cafe built from two First World War Army huts joined end to end. It was a massive place. On we went to Slough and used the recently opened North Circular Road to reach Tottenham.

Although the roads were still quite narrow there was only a small (a very small) fraction of today's traffic. There were, however, many more motorbikes and some of their riders used to swish past us far too close for comfort. We reached my uncle's at about three o'clock, after a thirty-mile ride on an almost empty North Circular Road, one of the country's first bypasses, completed a year or so before. Factories were springing up along the route — I have a memory of that belonging to Betta Biscuits, a somewhat short-lived company, who had cocked a snoot at the old established manufacturers by marketing a complete range of pound packets for only sixpence a time. Customers found them marvellous value and their advent must have affected sales by their competitors, but the profit margin (if any) was insufficient and Betta Biscuits vanished.

A wonderful tea awaited us, to which we did justice, and my uncle gave us no time to relax before taking us on a tour of the City, showing us many landmarks in what was, on that August Sunday, a virtual ghost town.

The next day we started for home at nine o'clock and decided to go back via the City and Chiswick to make the return trip more interesting. We made good time and hit Andover at about three. Just after reaching Weyhill, on a long straight stretch with little traffic, we saw a Morgan three-wheeler car approaching several hundred yards away. There was a bang and the vehicle lurched from side to side of the road before overturning. When after furious pedalling we reached the scene, several cars had already arrived and the driver of the Morgan, who had been thrown clear, was wandering around in a daze. The poor chap's shirt was hanging in tatters and his back was torn raw where he had been dragged along the gravel surface of the road. We all got together and managed to right the car, releasing his wife who was still underneath, lying unconscious. Someone drove off to phone for an ambulance, while the driver, who had recovered somewhat, kept repeating "My poor wife my poor wife". It seemed ages before the arrival of an ambulance from Andover, some five miles away, but by this time the wife was recovering consciousness. After we had helped push the car on to the verge we resumed our ride home, cogitating on the weakness of a three-wheeler, for the accident had been caused by a burst tyre on the single back wheel.

The London trip put us in good fettle for our holiday, some four weeks later, when we went off on a week's trip around Devon. Our timing was excellent as we did not have a spot of rain during the eight days that we were away. The Youth Hostels Association had been formed in 1932 and earlier in the year we had both become members, so were able to plan our tour staying at a different hostel at a cost of one shilling apiece each night. We left Salisbury on a Sunday morning and reached Wells by mid-afternoon. After viewing the Cathedral we went for tea at a Cyclist Touring Club-approved restaurant, where a meal for one shilling was guaranteed. At about five o'clock, we cycled the few miles to the youth hostel at Wookey Hole. This was a converted barn with about twenty bunk beds. We signed in (our membership number was always recorded in case of complaint of bad behaviour), drew our two blankets apiece, left our belongings on the beds and wandered off to see the caves. Next morning, we cooked breakfast on the gas ring (a penny in the slot meter) and made our way to Glastonbury Tor.

We had decided not to ride more than sixty miles each day to give us time to take in the countryside — and how we enjoyed it. Our target for that evening was Minehead, but we took time out at Watchet, intrigued by the tiny harbour. It was amazing to see all the coastal vessels stranded in a sea of mud at low tide. The youth hostel at Minehead was in the roof space of a laundry and had some thirty odd iron beds (possibly ex-army). The laundry was in a road on the side of a hill and entrance to the hostel was via a track running to the side and behind the building. This brought us up to the roof level and we had to cross a wooden footbridge to a tiny doorway, only some five feet six inches high, which was the only entrance and exit. What would have happened if fire had occurred heaven alone knows, fortunately I never read of a tragedy at the premises.

Next day, we had a fairly short run, as we wanted to stay at Bampton, so we had plenty of time to explore the lovely old town of Dunster. It was as well that we did give ourselves leeway because in early afternoon, when the sun was really blazing down, we came to a hill so steep that we dismounted and walked. We could see the corner in the distance and eventually reached it to find that the road continued climbing to another corner, almost half a mile away. On we walked, reached that corner, and still the road was climbing steeply. In all we walked over two miles until we finally reached a village called Wheddon Cross. We staggered into the one and only shop for refreshment and I shall never forget that place. It sold everything and hanging from the roof was footwear including ladies boots which had been out of fashion for more than twenty years. I went back to that shop in 1952 and it was much the same but the boots had gone. However, on my next visit in 1978 the proprietors seemed to have gone to town, as the shop was then an up-to-date mini-market!

When we reached Bampton, we found that the hostel was a medieval mill. The floorboards were oak planks some eighteen inches wide and three inches in thickness. There was the constant sound of rushing water. Men were on the top floor, ladies on the ground floor, strangely no doors separated the sexes, only an old oak staircase, but we didn't peep. How different to present day youth! Maybe we were born too early.

After tea we explored the tiny market town and I thought that Salisbury of 1850 must have looked much like it, with water running in channels at the side of the main streets, crossed by tiny footbridges. With a couple of other chaps from the hostel we went into a small old pub, and like men ordered a pint of cider apiece. It was served in double-handled pottery tankards and was the real thing, each mouthful really hitting the back of the throat. We sat at a table under the watchful eyes of the regulars and supped away. Not one of us drank more than half before we decided that the real Devon cider had defeated us, so we made our way out. I was the last to leave and glanced back to see that the old men, showing energy which I would never have believed they possessed, had jumped from their chairs, grabbed the tankards we had left with both hands, and were showing how cider should really be consumed.

The following day, Wednesday, we made our way down the beautiful Exe Valley to Exeter, then went immediately to Topsham, some four miles to the south of the city. The hostel there was the only one in that part of Devon and was very small, with accommodation for only six men and six women. The hosts ran a small farm, where stables provided sleeping quarters for the ladies while we were housed in the hayloft above, reached by outside wooden steps with handrail and having a landing at the top where there was a typical stable door, which allowed the top portion to be left open for ventilation. As soon as we had booked in (Topsham was one hostel where no advance booking was available) we were off back to spend the rest of the day in Exeter. During the afternoon, we passed a greengrocer's shop exhibiting some beautifully ripe purple plums, bought a pound apiece, then went to the recently opened Gaumont Palace, one of the South West's largest cinemas to see *F.P.1*. That must be one of the shortest titles on record and meant Floating Platform No 1, the story of an idea to have floating platforms, based in the Atlantic, where airliners could land and refuel. Sounds stupid now but it was only 1933.

At about eight o'clock we went back to Topsham, but on the way I began to feel somewhat queasy. By nine o'clock I expect I looked like death warmed up because an older cyclist staying at the hostel went to the farmer's wife and obtained a Seidlitz powder. After taking this, I went to bed and slept fitfully until about three o'clock, when I went out to the landing, leaned over the rail and was so sick I really thought I would die — I never wanted to see another plum again. I crept back to my bed, not really sleeping, for at the back of my mind was the thought I must rise early to clean up the mess. At six o'clock, I quietly got up and dressed, went out to the landing and looked down to the farmyard below. There was no sign of my mishap of early morning and the pigs were wandering around quite contentedly!

At breakfast, I took my place rather shamefaced, but fellow hostellers who must also have had a broken night due to my stupidity passed no comment. We left on our next stage, another easy one to Bridport. It was easy in mileage, although anyone knowing that road will remember one steep hill after another — but what wonderful scenery. The Bridport hostel was a private house belonging to a Mrs Reynolds. We had booked in some ten days earlier, as she only had room for four tourists. She gave us the choice of sleeping indoors or on camp beds in a tent, pitched on the lawn. We chose the tent as the nights were very hot. Mrs Reynolds, a very kind person, was typical of those who enabled the Youth Hostel Association to grow. They certainly did not carry out the work for money — the standard charge for a night's stay was only one shilling, which included the use of two blankets.

On Friday we left Bridport bound for Radipole, a suburb of

Weymouth, where we were to stay with my friend's grandparents. During the next day and a half we thoroughly explored the town, had a trip by train to Portland, found a shop which sold delicious fish and chips and still had enough money left to buy small gifts for those at home.

Sunday, the last day of a memorable week, saw us making our way home. It was still fine but now a strong wind was blowing in from the sea — it was so rough as we cycled along the coast road to Osmington that we were drenched several times by waves breaking over sea wall and my friend was sent headlong off his machine, fortunately without damage. When the sun got up, the wind dropped and approaching Wareham there were several fires burning on the scorched heathland. We made good time and reached home at about three o'clock. My mother took one look at me and said "You look just like a nigger". We had ridden over two hundred miles and had a fabulous time — all for the sum of two pounds apiece and at the end of it felt fit as fiddles.

I said that I was fit, but certainly didn't feel it when we played our first practice match of the soccer season a couple of weeks later. The muscles toned up by all the summer's cycling were the wrong ones needed for football and during the second half of that game I had a job to raise a gallop. However, the problem was short-lived, for in the next practice match against pretty tough opponents the tiredness had gone and I was ready for the first league match, a home fixture against Durrington.

This was a game that my father wanted us to win, for in the visitor's team were several workmates from his time at Heavers. It was played on a lovely September afternoon and the pitch was baked hard, making for a lively ball. That season we had the makings of a good side, but although having almost all the play and the advantage of the slope, we were losing by a goal to nil at half time. Shortly after the restart we equalised through Reg Roper but almost immediately Durrington broke away and scored, making it 1-2. We continued to dominate but the goalkeeper played an outstanding game and we could not score. Time was running out when Reg Roper ran on to my pass and drove home his second goal of the afternoon 2-2. With only two or three minutes left, the move was repeated, but this time Reg's shot was turned round the post

for a corner, which he took. We had a system for corners, the other
four forwards lined up on the edge of the penalty area and as the
ball was played in came forward in a rush which enabled us to
head the ball fairly and squarely. On this occasion, I was fortunate
and headed the ball out of the goalkeeper's reach and into the back
of the net. The next few moments are firmly imprinted in my mind,
for as I turned to go back to the centre circle I saw my father
standing on the touchline with his friends. As was usual he had
Peter, our Sealyham terrier with him. Now Dad was not an
excitable type but there he was, dancing around, waving his arms
and shouting his head off. It was a truly wonderful moment for me,
one that I still treasure.

After losing the third match of the season, we won the next seven
and topped the league at the beginning of December. Then our
hopes were shattered by three defeats. However, from January 6th
we went the rest of the season without losing another match and
meanwhile notched up thirty five goals while conceding only seven.
An inquest followed each game, for on Saturday evenings we would
meet at the George and Dragon inn in Castle Street and over half-
pints of cider or shandy would go over and over that afternoon's
match.

The after-match talks paid off, but invariably another topic crept
into the conversation, the threats being made by the German
Chancellor, Hitler. A couple of weeks into the football season, the
evening papers were plastered with headlines giving his latest
proclamation — he was leaving the League of Nations. I remember
the comment from our right half, Alf Stone, that by the next
season, we would all be in the Army. Just after this came the news
of the first concentration camps — of Jews being rounded up.

Nearer home, at a massive rally of Blackshirts, where the facist
salute was given, Sir Oswald Mosley called for the setting up of a
dictatorship. Despite the gloomy news we carried on enjoying life,
on very restricted incomes and tried to forget the threat of
Germany. Like most people in this country, we didn't want to know.

Chapter Eight 1934
The Guildhall murder that wasn't

On a Saturday morning in January, 1934, Salisbury awoke to the news of a murder at the city's Guildhall the previous evening. A private dance had been held, organised by the Bachelor's Club whose members, unattached males below the age of thirty five, used the occasion to reciprocate the hospitality which they had received during the previous year. Invitations to the yearly function were much sought after and security was tight.

The evening was ruined when several young men in their early twenties, seeing the lights and hearing the music emanating from the Guildhall, tried to gain entry. The three beadles on duty explained that it was a private function, admission was by invitation only, and refused them entry. Unfortunately, one of the uniformed officials was a pretty abrasive character and before long what started as good natured argument led to blows being exchanged. Augmenting the Guildhall staff that evening was the elder brother of one of the beadles, a very harmless individual who had unfortunately suffered a long period of unemployment owing to the recession. I knew him well because for several years he had helped with the running of our Scout troop. He was an extremely kind chap and I remember his dog — a Dalmation we called Plum Pudding. This inoffensive individual became the victim when, during the mêlée, he was struck an unfortunate blow by one of those wanting to gain entry. Poor M, who had been trying to keep out of trouble, fell backwards down the Guildhall steps, banged his head on the stone paving, fractured his skull and died a few minutes later.

The following morning (Saturday), J--- appeared at a special Magistrates' Court held in the Guildhall, charged with murder, which was then a capital offence, and was remanded in custody.

Over the next few months, he made periodic appearances which resulted in further remands, and eventually, after a lengthy hearing, the case was sent to the Spring Assizes. Imagine the state of the poor chap's mind as he spent day after day in his cell awaiting trial. Those of us who knew him held him in high regard, most definitely he was not and never had been a violent type. The city waited with bated breath as the days ticked by — the accused had the sympathy of most people, for he was as well thought of, as the poor victim had been. Both were members of greatly respected families.

The opening of the Assizes at that time was awe inspiring. After a Cathedral service, the judge would be driven fully robed, surrounded by a Cavalry escort wearing plumed helmets, to the Guildhall. As he entered, trumpeters on the steps sounded a fanfare and the square would be thronged with onlookers. On this occasion there were more sightseers than usual because of the interest in the local murder.

When the case was called, the prosecuting council started to outline the charge, but was soon halted by the judge, who suggested the accused could not be guilty of murder and that he should have been charged with manslaughter. J--- was then tried on the reduced charge. Later the judge indicated that he had no case to answer. J--- was then released after spending three months in custody facing a capital charge. In his remarks when discharging the prisoner, the judge said that he felt the wrong man stood in the dock — if anyone had to be charged, it ought to have been the one who started the fight. Everyone in the city was relieved at the outcome which was a happy ending to a most unfortunate occurrence.

My three-year apprenticeship had finished in December 1933, and early in the new year, my colleague, the only other employee, told me that Mr Gething had given him a week's notice. Work had not been too plentiful for some time and I had wondered how long things could go on unchanged. My colleague felt it was unfair that he should be the one to go, but Mr Gething was adamant and the next week gave me a rise in pay, albeit a small one. However, where there had been insufficient work for three, there seemed to be plenty for two and some overtime ensued.

At Easter, I almost had a surfeit of football — at Swindon on Good Friday, Porton on Saturday and Southampton on Monday. The Porton game was the last of our season and so we were free to go and watch the Saints at the Dell. We must have been keen, for it meant a forty-five mile cycle ride. How different things were in those days, people were much more honest. When we reached Southampton, the three of us made a beeline for a pub which was on the corner of Archer's Road, only two hundred yards from the entrance to the Dell. They had a large yard and we were allowed to leave our bikes in this for tuppence a time. It's true that the gatekeeper was a burly individual, but no tickets were given and the bikes were not identified. After the game we just went along, collected our bikes and there they were, no-one had tampered with them. Now they would need to be padlocked and even then safety is not ensured, for often the padlocks are cut.

The Saints sides of the Thirties fought a battle each season against relegation from the Second Division. From time to time, their best players had to be sold to obtain the wherewithal to pay summer wages. One of those who had to move was Ted Drake, one of the best centre forwards of all time. Southampton spotted him as a teenager, playing for Winchester City in the Hampshire League. Through his outstanding marksmanship, the Saints enjoyed a couple of their better seasons, then it was the same old story and off he had to go to Arsenal, where he won FA Cup Winners' medals, League Division I championship Medals and International Cups for England.

I remember a game in mid-April, 1934, when with two friends I cycled down to see the match of the season, against Grimsby, who had already won the Division II championship. We left work at one o'clock on a Saturday, started away at half past and arrived at the ground with about three minutes to go to kick-off time. Gates at that time averaged less than 10,000, but on that day I expect the attendance was more like 14,000. No-one gave the Saints much chance, they were struggling, as usual, towards the foot of the table. Half time score was 1-1 and Grimsby seemed to be on top. That year and for several more, they had a fine half back line, named Hall, Betmead and Buck, each man was a six-footer and all went on to League or International honours. Grimsby scored again, but in the last quarter of an hour the Saints banged in three, to win a memorable game by four goals to two. By now, there was a heavy drizzle. We collected our bikes from the pub yard and before we reached the outskirts of the town it was pouring with rain, which continued all the way home. We all got soaking wet, but we didn't care because the Saints' win had put us in high spirits. They were wonderful days!

In Spring, men's fancies, they say ... and so it was for me in May. A girl cousin of my cousins at Poole came to stay with us for a week. She arrived on Tuesday and by Friday I had courage enough to suggest a cycle ride. That evening she borrowed my sister's bike and off we went, thoroughly enjoying one another's company. We went out for a walk on Saturday and again on Sunday morning when we booked tickets for a coach mystery trip in the afternoon. It was a glorious day and we finished at Milford-on-Sea, wandered along the cliff-top and there had our first kiss. It was wonderful and on Monday, E--- (yes, the same initial as my first girlfriend) and I went for a walk, then to the second house performance at the Picture House. I saw her off by train on the Tuesday and we were both sad, for although she had agreed to return on Saturday we felt four whole days would be an eternity. It was, but at last the great day arrived — Whit Saturday. After dinner, I cycled down to Poole; what a journey, for not only was it cloudy but I faced a stiff head wind all the way. E--- left her work at six o'clock and after tea we cycled back to Salisbury — a rather easier journey with the wind behind us. Both Sunday and Monday produced the same sort of weather, so we returned to Poole by excursion train — the cost was three shillings return.

The romance lasted only nine weeks, but they were never to be forgotten. We saw one another each weekend. I usually cycled to Poole on Saturday, stayed overnight, then rode back late on Sunday evening. During the week, there were usually two letters in each direction — young love is wonderful. At the end of the nine weeks, E--- met a local boy (eventually, several years later, they were married) and I got the chop. The writing was probably on the wall a week earlier, when on a glorious Sunday morning E--- and I were walking along Poole Quay. She was looking like a million dollars in a beautiful new pale blue dress, crowned by a white straw picture hat. Suddenly the wind took a hand and the very fetching hat took off and floated gently into the sea. E--- stood, clutching her head and saying "Do something, do something". The thing that I did was unpardonable — I almost split my sides with laughter. An old boatman, face creased in smiles, said "I get 'un for ee, Missie" and fished it out with a boat-hook. Things became rather strained and this was possibly the beginning of the end. It hurt, but such is life.

That year, 1934, Salisbury hosted the Royal Counties Show. This was held in fields at Wilton Road, early in June. The show brought us a great deal of work from local firms who were exhibiting and this lead to welcome overtime, for I was still only receiving one pound, ten shillings a week.

The country had a wonderful boost during the first week of July, for during a cricket season dominated once again by the free-scoring Australians, England decisively won the Second Test at Lords. This victory was quickly followed by unparalleled success at Wimbledon when Fred Perry won the Men's and Dorothy Round, the Ladies' championships. It is very doubtful if this feat will ever be repeated.

Around this time we had another indication of Hitler's sadistic nature when we read of the episode which was to become known as "The night of the long knives". On his orders, many of his colleagues, some of whom had served him for years, were massacred. The operation was carried out by a Herr Himmler, who ten years later was notorious as the chief of the SS.

As my romance came to an end towards the end of July, I was at a loose end for my holiday, which I had booked for the last week in August. I wrote to my uncle in London, a civil servant who had the whole month for holiday, and was invited to spend the week with him. He was quite a character, a very quiet but deep individual. Everything he did was to a set pattern, his pocket watch was wound at nine o'clock each evening. I still have that watch, given him by George Herbert's School in Salisbury when he gave up his job as a pupil teacher in 1894 on entering the Civil Service. The winder is polished smooth by its constant winding.

On the first day of his summer holidays he would go to his tailor and order two navy blue serge suits, even though he probably had not worn the new ones from the previous year. Uncle Arthur had a wonderful brain and his analysis of world situations was very far sighted. During that holiday, we were sitting one evening on a tube train opposite two young German boys, who were excitedly reading the *Beobachter Zeitung*, Hitler's mouthpiece. After they had left the train he said "Either we stop Germany now or we shall have another World War in a few years time".

After living in London for forty years, twenty of them as a bachelor, he was a wonderful guide and quite an authority on the Wren churches in the City. During that week we must have visited most of them. Uncle also took me one evening to the East End to see Sidney Street, and told me that he had been in the crowd of spectators while the famous siege of 1911 was actually taking place.

The highlight of the week was our visit to Radiolympia, when we saw a demonstration of television for the first time. It's true the screen was minute and the silent pictures were terribly fuzzy, but it was a memorable experience and we queued for a long time to see it. I also have a vivid memory of M---'s stand, the first one inside the doors. They gave every visitor a large paper carrier bag, which was bright yellow and printed on this in brilliant red was the firm's trademark.

The object of the exercise was to enable all visitors to trudge around the massive exhibition and use the carrier bag to store the mountains of literature available, at the same time publicising M---s radio sets. A wonderful advertising gimmick that went badly wrong, because the yellow ink used to print the background was not fast and came off on the hands, from the hands to the face and everything that was touched. The sides of my trousers were so marked with yellow, from the rubbing of the bag against them as I walked, that the only answer was dry cleaning. If the visitors had banded together and sued for compensation, I would imagine the damages might have ruined the company, although seeing all the yellow hands, yellow streaked faces and yellow trousers, there was a funny side. However, the day re-awakened my interest in radio — several years earlier I had made both a crystal and a one-valve set. During the afternoon, I remember newsvendors, rushing around Olympia, shouting "Test Match Result". Few people bought the papers as the result was a foregone conclusion. Once again, Australia had regained the Ashes and apart from the Lords' test, which England won convincingly, had really wiped the floor with the home country.

On the following Saturday, which was the opening of the football season, my uncle and I went over to White Hart Lane where Tottenham were playing Everton. It was a privilege to be present, as the visitors scored the only and winning goal in the first minute, before one Tottenham player touched the ball. Involved in the move were three great English internationals, the full back Warnie Cresswell, then approaching retirement, Cliff Britton, at right half, and possibly one of the greatest centre forwards of all time, Dixie Dean. Everton kicked off. The ball was passed back to Cresswell, who laid it to Cliff Britton, who took a few paces forward and put a long, high lob towards the Tottenham penalty area, where Dixie Dean rose high above the defenders and with a flick of the head put the ball into the net. It was all so simple, but disastrous for Tottenham, who never recovered from the shock, were relegated and did not gain promotion until 1950.

At the end of August, the engagement of Prince George to Princess Marina of Greece was announced. The wedding took place later in the year. This was to have a profound effect on the nation, as over the next year or so numerous baby girls were christened Marina, but the fashion for the name was short-lived. We now find ladies called Marina are invariably approaching their sixtieth birthdays.

As far as my own football was concerned, I had played my last competitive game. Towards the end of the previous season, a collision of heads left me with slight concussion which lasted for a couple of days. In the next match against Porton, I headed a quite heavy ball and collapsed for a few minutes, being again concussed. As a result, Dr Gordon suggested that I gave up the game. But even now, the best part of sixty years on, the sight of a football can still give me itchy feet.

My birthday (September 22nd) of that year is remembered as a black day, owing to the mining disaster that occurred early that morning at Gresford, near Wrexham. The Wrexham Football Club had an important home match that afternoon, so far more miners than usual were working on the Friday night shift, in order that they would be free to attend the match. There was an explosion and almost three hundred men were entombed. We heard via the wireless of the efforts to reach them and several would-be rescuers were also killed. When the evening papers came out, there were pages of pictures of distressing scenes at the pithead. The whole nation went into mourning. As far as Salisbury was concerned, the incident must have been quickly forgotten as a band of charitably minded people who put on a fund-raising whist drive and dance at the Guildhall, in aid of the Gresford Disaster Fund, did not take enough money to pay expenses and were left to foot the bill.

As I felt quite lost without my football on Saturdays I had to find a new interest and turned to radio. While still at school I had made a crystal set, now I ventured further and produced a two-valve receiver. This was entirely made from secondhand parts, bought for a song from Clayton's Fisherton Street shop, which the firm kept for radio repairs. From this small beginning, I next made the latest four-valve receiver, the ST600, which had been designed by John Scott-Taggart. The cost of this put me in hock for many weeks but it really was a powerful set with a moving coil loudspeaker, the latest thing in 1934 technology.

That winter, I also signed on, with two of my friends, for carpentry classes. These were held at the Handicraft Centre in Brown Street and were most instructive and enjoyable. Over the years, I had already learnt a great deal about working in wood from Dad and his friends. Now, under Mr Stevens, I was able to put the knowledge to good use. We were allowed to make whatever we wished and within a few weeks I had produced a bookcase with cupboard underneath, which fitted into an alcove in my bedroom. Some of the chaps who were courting were busily engaged in making furniture, for there was an added bonus in working at the evening class — all the timber was sold to us at half price.

My next effort was a modern cabinet for the radio that I was busily constructing. It was of real art deco design and when I look back and think about it I shudder, for it was far too large, being about four feet, six inches high and two feet, six inches wide. How tastes change with the years.

Then my uncle, who was to retire from the Civil Service the following year and hoped to return to Salisbury, heard of my efforts and asked if I would make a kitchen table. This took me many weeks and was a most solid job with a one-and-a-quarter-inch deal top and a drawer at either end. Although I only spent one year at the Handicraft Centre, I learnt much which has been useful to me in the years that have followed and I still find pleasure in going into my workshop to produce things in wood — it's a lovely hobby.

In November, the His Master's Voice show train was parked in Salisbury Station for a few days. It was a Radiolympia in miniature and was visited by thousands of people eager to see the latest sets and discuss points with experts. Looking back, the giant strides that had been taken in the radio industry in twelve short years, both in receivers and transmission, were quite amazing. Now we were able to listen regularly to foreign programmes and there was even a magazine, *World Radio,* which listed these. It was a far cry from the crystal sets of the Twenties.

True, some fifty per cent of sets were still powered by high-tension batteries and low-tension accumulators. A 120 volt battery might cost about twelve shillings and sixpence and have a life of perhaps three months if you were lucky. The performance of the battery, and thus the the volume of the set, deteriorated gradually from its first day of use. Accumulators had to be recharged at regular intervals, usually once a week. The recharging was a profitable sideline for numerous businesses such as garages, cycle shops and general stores. One or two keen traders even ran a collection and delivery service. It was always necessary to have at least two accumulators, one in use and one on charge. The cost for this was sixpence, showing a profit of about six hundred per cent.

Those lucky enough to possess a supply of mains electricity were spared the frustration of settling down to enjoy a favourite programme, then being let down by battery failure. It made even strong men weep to have to put an ear right against the loud speaker to catch ever diminishing sound.

Chapter Nine 1935
I go on police records

I've said little about the way that Salisbury was changing in the late Twenties and through the Thirties. Just after the First World War council houses made their first appearance, in the Macklin Road area. Then in the mid-Twenties more were built on allotments between Laverstock Road and Wain-a-Long Road. After this there was ribbon development when the Council built houses at the top of Devizes Road opposite Highbury Avenue and extending almost to Roman Road. Still more appeared on the fair field in Castle Road, where firstly Waters Road and then Fairfield Road were built. At the same time, after the extension of Ashley Road and the erection of a narrow bridge of one vehicle width over the River Avon, which linked up with Butts Road, still more houses were built to become Douglas Haig Road.

It was not only the Council which was active, private developers were also enlarging the city in all directions. The fields on the right hand side of Castle Road, over a mile in length, vanished very quickly. Housing on Devizes Road was extended by another mile, much of the area between Wilton Road and Devizes Road was filled in, as were sites at Harnham and Coombe Road. In 1935, a small estate of bungalows built in Southampton Road (now Tollgate Road) was christened Marina Road, in honour of the new Duchess of Kent.

Many names of the speculative building fraternity of that era spring to mind — Wort and Way, Bundy, Porter, Gunstone, Lailey and Forder. Between them they must have built as many new houses as had been put up in Salisbury in the previous hundred and fifty years. At one time a house was available for a deposit of £35 (a bungalow for £25) and a mortgage was generally spread over twenty years. The cost of houses varied from £575 to £1,000 and a semi-detached bungalow could be obtained for £375. Many stories were circulating of the jerry building that was supposed to be rife, but the houses are still there some sixty years on, and fetching prices (even allowing for inflation) that make the original cost seem a greater bargain than ever.

The city centre too was gradually changing. For many years one of the police chores was point duty on the crossroads at Blue Boar Row and Queen Street and at Milford Street and Queen Street. At peak times, St Ann's Street and Exeter Street were also manned. An experimental set of traffic lights was installed at the Milford Street and Queen Street junction, operated by a mat to make the lights change. Lights at the other two junctions followed and shortly afterwards additional ones appeared to ease the traffic along from London Road to Bournemouth and Southampton. It seemed as though sleepy Salisbury was really entering the twentieth century.

In the Twenties, Fisherton Street had been a principal shopping street, people making their way to and from the railway stations ensuring a constant stream of would-be customers. Now, road transport was taking over, and bus and haulage companies grew apace at the expense of the railway, which lost most of its short-haul patrons. No longer did country people flock into the city on Market Day and Saturday railway excursions. The number of sheep and cattle arriving at Milford Station was rapidly diminishing as the much more convenient lorries delivered their loads direct to the market and auction marts. This door-to-door service was also given to people by the ever growing bus companies and although many carriers continued in business until the advent of the Second World War, most of them gave up the unequal struggle and sold out to the Wilts and Dorset company.

In the city itself, for several years, there was extremely fierce competition between Victory Coaches, owned by Sparrow and Vincent, and the larger firm of Wilts and Dorset. The rivalry was such that both companies invested in fourteen-seater buses, nicknamed "chasers". Although no accidents happened, the behaviour of some drivers of these vehicles was quite reprehensible. They would follow one another through the city, and when they reached a stopping place, the second driver would rush the business of descending passengers as quickly as possible, then start away, passing his competitor who was picking up the waiting public. On to the next stop and the operation would be done in reverse. Rivalry on the summer excursions to the coast was especially keen, for in addition to the companies running the two city bus services, Rowlands ran some half a dozen coaches on a regular basis. The return fare to Bournemouth, was slashed to two shillings, children from five to sixteen half price, under-fives free of charge (but they were expected to ride on a parent's lap). It was sheer madness and no-one could have made much money.

Eventually the railways borrowed large sums of money from the Government at an extremely low rate of interest. These funds, intended for modernisation, were instead used to buy up bus companies, with the object of producing a monopoly. In 1931, the Southern Railway became a major shareholder of the Wilts and Dorset Bus Company.

The following year, Sparrow and Vincent's Victory Coaches were absorbed by Wilts and Dorset and three years later, Rowlands were also swallowed up. The cost of excursions to Bournemouth soon reverted to three shillings and sixpence, but I have to admit that thanks largely to Mr Ray Longman, the managing director of the Wilts and Dorset Company (he had started life as an estate agent), Salisbury and District now had a bus service second to none. It was true that some drivers were only engaged for the summer season and spent most winters on the dole, but that's how life was in the Thirties.

As far as shopping was concerned, Silver Street, the New Canal and Blue Boar Row came into much more prominence, the two latter because they were bus stops for most parts of the city. In 1933, Moore Brothers, the very old established boot makers, moved from Silver Street to the Canal and were replaced by Timothy Whites. The following year, Marks & Spencer's small bazaar in Minster Street closed and the firm moved to spacious new premises next to Timothy Whites. Fifty Shilling Tailors came to the city when they bought the premises of Snooks the butchers (again old established), on the corner of Silver Street and High Street. I remember that when they opened one of the models in the window was of a very happy looking man, about five feet two inches tall, with a girth of the same measurement. It was a real figure of fun and we all thought he was most amusing, something that I am sure was not shared by any men of similar build. I think Fifty Shilling Tailors must possibly have had complaints for the model vanished.

There also seemed to be an influx of multiple footwear shops, so many that when it was announced that another was coming, a friend remarked "What do they think we are in Salisbury — b----- centipedes". Although during this period, numerous old established city businesses splashed out and gave themselves a new look with modern shop fronts, there was little building in the centre. One exception during the mid-Twenties had been the Co-operative Society's headquarters in Winchester Street, and Boots the Chemists rebuilt their premises on the corner of The Canal and High Street. A few old faces vanished — Fowler and Bailey, the Catherine Street drapers, was taken over by Walter Dunthorne. The jewellers Sly's, who had moved from Blue Boar Row (where they had been trading for many, many years) to Queen Street, closed as did the Domestic Bazaar Company in Silver Street. Generally there was little change and life moved at the same slow pace as befitted a cathedral city.

Early in 1935, a friend introduced me to the joys of motor-bikes. He lived at Downton and was having great fun with a couple of mates enjoying grass-track thrills on an old machine on Barford Down. I went along several times. We used to pick up the bike, which was left in a barn on a farm nestling at the foot of the downs, and had hours of good fun. I was hooked, so thought about buying a machine of my own and with my Downton friend made several visits to Pepperells in Cherry Orchard Lane. One evening I bought a 350cc Zenith, several years old but it went. The following Saturday, we pushed it (it was uninsured and not licensed) to a private road at Milford which led on to Clarendon. There we tried out the bike, taking it in turns to ride the half mile or so of gravel track. I was making the return trip, thoroughly enjoying myself, when, as I went up the hill, I saw two uniformed police with my friend. One, a constable, stepped out majestically and held up his hand.

"Do you have a road fund licence for this machine?" he asked. "No." "Do you hold a driving licence?" "No." Out came his note book and I had to give all my details — name, address, occupation. The bobby did all this under the eagle eye of his colleague, a chief inspector. Off they went and we ruefully pushed the bike back to Salisbury. When I arrived home and told the story, oh dear! oh dear! oh dear! Had I committed murder my parents could not have been more upset.

"None of my family has ever been mixed up with the police." Mum said MY family — this was a dig at poor old Dad for his great-great uncle had appeared at the Dorchester Assizes charged with deer-stealing at Donhead St Mary, "within the confines of Cranborne Chase". Both he and his son were ordered to be transported to Australia for seven years. According to the Australian Association of Donhead Descendants, the father returned to this country. During his absence the High Court ruled that Donhead was not within the Chase and, although no pardon was given, they were not guilty of the crime.

I was made to feel a criminal and the first thing I had to do was get rid of "that damned bike". I quickly sold it, then waited for nemesis to arrive. The weeks went by, then on a Saturday lunchtime, I arrived home and when I walked in my mother didn't say anything but just pointed over her shoulder, towards the mantelpiece. There, propped up against the clock, was an official looking folded blue paper. I opened it and there were two pieces of paper, each a summons to appear at the District Petty Sessions to be holden at the Guildhall on the following Tuesday week. One referred to my lack of insurance, the other to my lack of a driving licence. My mother was quite cross, because the summonses had been delivered by a constable in uniform, "the first time we've ever had the police knock at our door".

Dad went that evening to pay a visit to an old friend, a sergeant in the city police, to find out the best way to deal with the matter and Walter, the friend, said: "I wonder what a chief inspector was doing in that out of the way spot — I'll find out. Tell your boy to write and plead guilty say it won't happen again and that he didn't know that he needed a driving licence and insurance on a private road. Ignorance of the law is no plea, but it should help them to deal lightly."

A few days later he saw Dad and told him that the police had been in that area because there had been a serious burglary at Wilton and word had come through that two suspicious looking men had been seen in the Laverstock area. How unlucky can you be? With the help of my sister, I duly wrote the suggested letter, delivered it to the Magistrates' Clerk's Office by hand and waited for the police to arrive and cart me off to jail! (I'm sure my mother thought that's what would happen). Instead, when I got home for tea on that fateful Tuesday evening, a letter was waiting, informing me that I had been fined five shillings in each case. I was so relieved that I collected two friends and treated them both to the pictures, followed by a fish and chip supper. However, the agony wasn't over, for on Friday, my misdemeanour was reported in the *Salisbury Times*, the *Salisbury Journal*, the *Western Gazette* and the *Southern Evening Echo*. My mother said: "I shall never be able to hold my head up again."

That year, my brother-in-law, being an old friend of the Wiltshire Football Association secretary, managed to get hold of two cup final tickets. The game was played on Saturday, April 27th between Sheffield Wednesday and West Bromwich Albion. We left Salisbury by train on Friday evening and were met at Waterloo by my uncle, who had kindly offered us accommodation. We were up early on Saturday, went into the city by tube and surfaced for an hour or so before making our way to Wembley. London, already decorated in readiness for King George V's Silver Jubilee, to be held nine days later on Monday, May 6th, was ablaze with blue and white. Unfortunately, both clubs sported the same colours (although West Bromwich played in their change strip of white that day).

When we arrived at Wembley station we had about a mile to walk to the stadium and all traffic on the road was stopped to make sure that the crowds arriving by every train could make the journey on foot. I remember being amazed by the number of police employed — they were standing a few yards apart in the centre of the road all the way to the ground and making a good job of keeping the multitude on the move. Our seats were quite expensive, costing seven shillings and sixpence, and when we reached them I was glad that I had borrowed my father's pocket binoculars, for we must have been a hundred yards from the nearest touchline. I consider myself fortunate in having attended a

Cup Final, because it is a wonderful experience. In the Thirties, community singing was in vogue and people of my generation showed great respect — the massive stadium was hushed before the hymn *Abide with Me* and everyone stood to attention for the National Anthem. I can imagine many of the modern generation dismissing this with "Silly old fools" — I feel it is a great pity that this sort of respect has all but vanished. There were a hundred thousand people there that day, which passed without any signs of the hooliganism so prevalent today.

The game itself started in sensational fashion, when in the first minute "Sausage" Palethorpe, the Wednesday centre forward, swept the ball past the West Brom keeper, Pearson, to open the scoring. I was ecstatic, I wanted Sheffield to win. Phil, my brother-in-law, was down in the dumps — he was rooting for the other side. Shortly afterwards, an incident occurred which I can still see clearly, fifty-six years on, it was so amusing. The referee that day, while having a reputation as a disciplinarian, was the smallest on the League list and was under five feet six inches. He had already whistled for a foul by the West Brom half back Murphy, when the same player offended for the second time. He called him over and gave him a thorough lecture, wagging his finger all the while. Murphy, who was about six feet two, towered over the official, but looked rather like a naughty boy. The incident was captured by a press photographer and appeared in the Sunday papers, under the headline "Dignity and Impudence".

After half an hour West Brom equalised, then Wednesday got another goal and so the score remained until, with only some ten minutes of the game left, Sandford, the West Brom inside left who had first appeared in the 1931 final as a seventeen-year-old, managed at last to beat Brown, the Wednesday goalkeeper. To me the latter had always been a hero, for I remembered reading about him when, in 1923, playing for Worksop Town as a teenager, he kept a clean sheet against Tottenham Hotspur at White Hart Lane in the third round of the Cup. It was real *Boys Own Paper* stuff — sadly Tottenham won the replay by 9-0 but Brown was established, joined Wednesday, and by 1935 was something of a veteran. Now, in the final, he played a prominent part in a never-to-be-forgotten victory. When only five minutes of the game remained, West

LEFT: Catherine Street decorated for the Silver Jubilee of King George V and Queen Mary. Note the Victorian gas lamp standard. Salisbury at long last went all-electric a week prior to the outbreak of the Second World War, only for the new lighting to be switched off for more than five years.

BELOW: A horse-drawn entry in the Silver Jubilee procession on May 6th, 1935, with Rueben Davis and his son George. The sun shone from dawn to dusk, in direct contrast to the torrrential rain during the 700th anniversary celebrations eight years earlier.

Bromwich, now playing well and looking much the better side, forced a corner. The ball came across the goal and was caught by Brown, who booted it well upfield where Rimmer, the Wednesday outside left, fastened on to it and was away with half the field clear, for the opposing defenders were caught in the Sheffield penalty area, having all gone up to try and force a goal.

Rimmer sped on. Pearson came out, but could do nothing to stop the winger, who scored easily. Strangely, within another two minutes, Wednesday made the score 4-2 with a repeat performance. Again their opponents forced a corner. Again Brown, using his safe pair of hands, caught the ball. Again he booted it up the field to where Rimmer was waiting in a wide open space, and again Pearson had no chance with the winger's shot.

I recall the goalkeeper picked the ball out of the net and was going to kick it upfield; instead he turned round and booted it back in the net in sheer disgust, knowing that he, like his father before him, would only receive a loser's medal. It was an amazing finish and one could only feel sorry for the West Bromwich side, who had played well enough to have won. It was to be another nineteen years before they achieved a win at Wembley.

We waited in our seats for almost an hour to allow the crowd to partly disperse, but it was still another hour and a half before we reached the city and a much needed meal. Then it was off to a news cinema to watch highlights of the game — my brother-in-law insisted that we saw it three times, so that I arrived back in Tottenham absolutely dog-tired after a quite wonderful day.

The following week was very hectic workwise, for the traders in Salisbury suddenly woke up to the fact that the King's Silver Jubilee was to be celebrated on the following Monday, when an excellent programme had been arranged. I remember having to work overtime each evening, all day on Saturday and most of Sunday to produce display material. Two items stand out in my memory, relating to vehicles entered by a garage for the grand procession. One was a giant "L" plate — driving tests had just been introduced. The second was in connection with the speed limit of 30mph in built up areas that was now enforceable. I remember

having to write, in three-inch letters, a ditty that was heard daily
on the radio:

> *I'm Gertie, the girl with the gong,*
> *I watch your cars speeding along,*
> *If you do more than thirty,*
> *Then Gertie gets shirty,*
> *And tinkles away on her gong.*

The morning of Monday, May 6th dawned as a glorious sunny
day. My mother asked me to decorate the outside of the house and
similar displays were everywhere. My sister even made a bow from
Silver Jubilee Blue ribbon for Peter, our Sealyham terrier to wear,
something which he did with great pride for he loved to be the
centre of attention. The churches were packed for the special
Services of Thanksgiving, people held the King in great affection
for he had led the country through the greatest war in history and
through the uneasy years of peace that followed.

The afternoon was taken up by a football match at Victoria Park
between Salisbury and Southampton Boys, and other entertainments
including boxing, bowls, miniature golf and band concerts. It was,
of course, a public holiday and for once the weather was kind. In
the evening, a grand procession trundled through the city as it
made its way to Victoria Park, where the day ended in dancing,
followed by a firework display.

On the following Monday, I met a young lady who a couple of
years later became my first wife. She was a Romsey girl, working at
Wilton, and my life suddenly became centred around what is now
an old-fashioned word, courting. I got to know all the walks around
Wilton, Grovely Woods, Bishopstone Hill, The Avenue and many
others. Neither of us had much money but we enjoyed many happy
outings and within a few weeks had visited each other's homes.
Romsey, of course, I knew well from my earlier visits to my aunt,
who had died in 1932. In that period before the war, it seemed a
run-down sort of town, with very few shops even approaching a
modern image. It had more than its share of unemployment and it
showed. The young lady, Gwen, was one of a large family, having
four sisters and three brothers, so the first visit to meet the family
was somewhat daunting. Her mother was proud of an uncle who
had served as mayor of the borough, many years before. One of her

brothers possessed a Morris saloon car. Although several years old it ran well and to me seemed the height of luxury. He also possessed the latest radio and was for ever up to some money-making scheme or another to supplement his shop assistant's wages. I always found him a likeable chap.

Courting in the Thirties was so different from the Nineties. Both parties respected each other and there was not the same desire to jump into bed at the earliest possible moment. Occasionally there were shot-gun weddings and reports in the local papers of men being sued in court for maintenance in respect of a male/female child born to so and so. These paternity cases usually resulted in an order for a weekly sum of seven shillings and sixpence to be paid until the child reached the age of fourteen. The poor unmarried mother was ostracised by neighbours, had the responsibility of bringing up a child on a pittance and would find employment most difficult to obtain. No wonder that so many people waited for marriage.

During the August Bank Holiday I suffered an accident which meant I went around with my left arm in a sling for several days. Playing football with the dog (he played with one ball in his mouth and used both front feet to control the other ball) I went a purler on the concrete yard, stuck out my arm to save myself and sprained my wrist. I felt a fool when I had to fill in a National Health Insurance form which asked "reason for' accident" with "playing football with dog". Strangely my explanation was accepted without comment.

During the autumn a gentleman arrived who was to have quite an impact on the city. The well established drapery house of Style and Gerrish (it was founded in 1803) was privately owned by the two daughters of the late Mr Richard Gerrish. After his death, it had been run by two men who continued to manage as though it was still a pre-First World War shop. As a result, Style and Gerrish was very much in the doldrums. A shopwalker, dressed in frock coat, an anachronism for 1935, could still be seen, ushering important customers into the shop, then snapping his fingers and saying "Forward, Miss ----". Now, a general manager was appointed, one with plenty of experience of modern department stores to bring the business up to date. Mr Richard Nowell came to Salisbury from

Plymouth, where he had been assistant manager of Spooners, the large Debenhams store.

Within a few weeks of his arrival, a difference could be seen. One of the first appointments he made was a new window dresser and soon the store was entering and winning national display competitions. Before long, new shop fronts gave it a very different image and many new items of merchandise were stocked. I remember that when flower bulbs were first displayed, a certain prominent seed merchant in the city threatened he would start stocking camiknickers. What a pity it was only an idle threat, it might have been interesting. Under "Dickie" Nowell a sale became an event, as proclaimed on the one hundred-odd-foot long sign, made of canvas (in twelve-foot sections) on wooden frames, that was erected all along the parapet, towering above the Market Place. For the next four years, I wrote at least three of these signs each year. I was also given the job of designing a new trademark, which made its appearance on paper bags, carrier bags, on plaques in the window, in all advertising, on the sides of the firm's vans and even in the hearse! Dickie gave the entire place a new look and not

Salisbury's Greatest Bargain Event was proclaimed by Salisbury's largest sign — one of the many the author wrote for Style and Gerrish (now Debenhams) in the Thirties.

only outside, for soon partitions and walls dating back to Victorian times and before were swept aside. On one occasion when this operation was under way, there was panic when movement was noticed on the second floor before a steel girder could be inserted, resulting in the clearance of everyone from the building. Fortunately it was a false alarm.

From 1936 on, until the intervention of wartime restrictions, the Style and Gerrish Christmas rides were a feature much loved by the kiddies. One year it was "By submarine to Father Christmas" — a wonderful treat and most realistic, for the children entered the "submarine", took their seats and watched as fish and other sea creatures floated past a small window at the front, all the while the sub was rocking slowly from side to side. When the engine stopped, the kiddies trooped through a door on the opposite side, where Father Christmas waited in a cave. On the day that he arrived at the store, thousands turned out to welcome him as he rode from the railway station on a horse-drawn sleigh, having apparently made the journey from London on "The Atlantic Coast Express". In reality the train slowed to a halt just before reaching Salisbury Station. An agile younger version of Santa was pushed aboard, the train continued the two hundred or so yards to the platform and the eager reception committee of youngsters. On arrival at the store, he climbed a ladder to one of the first floor windows, pausing to wave to his fans. The cheering really brought a lump to the throat.

At long last, in mid-1935, the country woke up to the ever growing menace of Hitler's Germany and the Government put plans in hand to enlarge the Air Force. As a result of this policy, the stone quarries at Chilmark, which supplied the stone for Salisbury Cathedral and had been used since Roman times, were purchased for conversion to an underground armaments dump. This meant a great deal to the area as it provided much needed employment for the local population.

Throughout the summer, another dictator, Mussolini, was making aggressive noises threatening the invasion of Abyssinia to give Italy breathing space. Although almost all members of the League of Nations deprecated his policy the Duce ignored them and on October 3rd put his plans for war into operation. The League applied sanctions against Italy and for a time, the poorly armed Abyssinians, led by their Emperor, Haille Selassie, seemed to be holding their own. In this country, a deal hatched by Sir Samuel Hoare, the Foreign Secretary and the French Premier, Pierre Laval, to appease Mussolini was thrown out by the Government and Hoare was forced to resign. His successor, Mr Anthony Eden, was to become one of the country's leading statesmen during the next twenty years. After months of fighting, during which Italy used her air power against an almost defenceless country, poison gas was employed and this proved to be decisive. The Emperor and his court fled to this country and the League of Nations sanctions were seen to be a complete failure. Mussolini's success encouraged Hitler, who started to increase his own rearmament and spelt the death knell of the League from which so much had been expected.

Chapter Ten 1936
Will Wally be Queen?

While this Abyssinian war was progressing, the British Empire suffered an enormous loss, when just over eight months after the wonderful Jubilee celebrations, the King died on Monday, January 20th, 1936. Less than a month before, he had given his usual Christmas Radio message and had only been ill for a few days — the first news coming on Friday the 17th. I remember that on that Monday evening, I caught the ten o'clock bus back from Wilton and on reaching home was greeted by my mother and father, both wearing grave expressions as they listened to the solemn music from the radio. One of them said: "The King is dying." Every ten minutes or so came an announcement in sombre tones: "The King's life is moving peacefully towards its close." We all remained gathered round the radio, drinking innumerable cups of tea; it was as if we were waiting for the death of one of the family. Then just after midnight came the announcement that he had died. I had never known another king and like millions of others went to bed very saddened.

The next morning the papers were full of pictures of the great events that had taken place during the seventy years of the King's life. Radio programmes took on a subdued and sombre mood. On the Wednesday, Edward was proclaimed King — the proclamation in Salisbury being read from the Guildhall steps by the Mayor as chief citizen.

One man, I remember, put all niceties to one side and made himself a small fortune. He was a small draper and a prominent member of the Chamber of Commerce. On the morning after the King's death, he went round the city canvassing other traders, then went to the Labour Exchange, offered temporary work to an unemployed painter and proceeded to supply black boards, made from six by three-quarter-inch deal, for erection on shop fronts. He also had several ladies producing black arm bands, which had a ready sale with the public. It's an ill wind . . .

Later in the week the press gave us pictures of the journey from Sandringham to Westminster Hall for the King's lying-in-state. The new King said that he did not wish all work to stop on the day of the funeral, but nevertheless almost every business in Salisbury closed until 3.30pm and a two-minute silence was observed.

Gwen and I went to the afternoon service in the Cathedral and then upset my mother by going to see a film at the Gaumont Palace when they opened at six o'clock. For us it was real relaxation after the restrictions of the previous week.

During the following month, we, as a family, moved house, thus breaking an eighty-year connection with Culver Street. The new house in Albany Road was quite a step up, for it not only had a bathroom, but also a hall and a rear entrance. No longer did cycles have to be lifted through two rooms. It was all very convenient. There was just one extra living room, but the splendid window of the kitchen in our former house was sadly missing. The new home was the typical late Victorian/Edwardian/Georgian (pre World War I) of which so many examples can be seen in almost every town and city in the country. Instead of being surrounded by artisans, we now had white collar workers as neighbours. Dad stopped wearing his overalls and sported a trilby hat when he went to work. One neighbour even possessed his own car and was a member of the City Council. It was all quite a departure.

At Easter, Mr Gething moved to quite convenient premises, just around the corner at No 4 Brown Street. He rented the first and second floors of a warehouse, above a food store. Each room was twenty feet square and the beauty of the place was the windows, which went the whole side of each room facing the street and were glazed with frosted glass. For the first time, I was working on a bench, eighteen feet in length, which made production of large work much easier. For some reason best known to my employer, the move took place on Easter Saturday, resulting in morning-long traffic jams in Winchester Street and much cursing from the poor police trying to keep things moving. In the new premises we also had a machine called a Cutawl, which enabled displays to be cut out very quickly. It was a very ingenious piece of equipment, working rather like a sewing machine with a chisel instead of a needle, with a head that was easily manoeuvred to follow a line at a speed of about two feet per minute.

During May, the new liner Queen Mary made her maiden voyage to Southampton and thousands, including myself went to see her before she sailed. She looked enormous and quite magnificent.

Civil War broke out in Spain in July and was to last for almost three years. At first, it seemed of no concern to us in Salisbury but was brought closer home when refugee camps were set up near Southampton Water. The two Axis powers gave full support to the rebel leader Franco and doubtless they regarded the war as a dress rehearsal for the real thing. An International Brigade was formed to support the Spanish Government and an appeal for men to join the force was made in Salisbury Market Place.

A veteran of the First World War who had been decorated for gallantry, then in his fifties and living quietly in the district, heard the call and fortunately returned unscathed. That chap really hated the Germans. There were also local appeals for clothing, bedding and cash. We had the uneasy feeling that it was Spain today, Britain tomorrow.

In late August, Gwen and I spent a week at Poole staying with my cousin and her husband, with whom we had a life-long friendship, but my outstanding memory is of the typhoid epidemic which had started just prior to our arrival. In the middle of the week I developed a very sore throat and was scared that I had become a typhoid victim, but after about twenty four hours I returned to normal. The source of the epidemic was traced to untreated milk being supplied by one farm. Apart from that hiccup it was a lovely holiday.

When Edward VIII became King in January, almost all my generation felt that a new era had dawned. He seemed so wonderful, a handsome sportsman who had never been afraid to risk his neck by riding in steeplechases and a keen supporter of youth movements, including the Scouts. He appeared almost god-like, but having what Rudyard Kipling called "the common touch". Just before his father's death, when visiting miners' cottages in

South Wales, he showed the caring side of his character by stating in no uncertain fashion that something must be done.

In the summer of 1936, we were all shocked to hear and read of an assassination attempt on his life by a Scottish journalist, but the authorities did not take the case very seriously as the man only received a year's imprisonment.

Then, in late October, when preparations for the King's Coronation to be held the following May were well advanced, rumours began to circulate in the country of Edward's liaison with a twice-divorced American lady. In fact the rest of the world had been informed of this for about a year — we were the last to know because of a voluntary ban on the news, imposed by the press barons.

For myself, I was quite unaware of the bombshell that was shortly to drop until on a visit to Romsey in late October, when my future father-in-law told me of what he had read in an American paper. I was quite scornful, so off he went to borrow the paper from a friend to prove his point. There it was, a banner headline in type about two inches high "Will Wally be Queen?". Below was a photograph of the lady with a crown superimposed on her head. The article went on to give chapter and verse of the couple's meetings, of Mrs Wallis Simpson's former marriages and much more. To say that I was shocked would be a gross understatement. I arrived home late that evening and blurted out the terrible news to my father, whose reaction was totally predictable — "If you believe that then you'd believe anything". Several weeks went by and we heard nothing more, so I began to think that my father's doubts on the story were well founded.

Then, in late November, the Bishop of Bradford preached a sermon in which he referred to the talk in foreign newspapers and said he wished His Majesty showed "more signs of awareness". The sermon was reported in *The Yorkshire Times* and suddenly the floodgates opened for the national press. Fleet Street made a meal of the story so long suppressed and every paper published on December 3rd left readers in no doubt of the seriousness of Edward and Mrs Simpson's liaison. Eight days of controversy followed, with the Prime Minister, Mr Stanley Baldwin, in the driving seat. Public opinion seemed to be split — the King had been so popular.

Edward could see no objection to a morganatic marriage. Baldwin said it was out of the question.

In 1936, divorce was still a dirty word, but a woman twice divorced was even more tainted and few wanted the forty-year-old Mrs Simpson as Queen. The Prime Minister consulted the premiers of all the Dominions and they were unanimous that the King's marriage to the lady was impossible. If he persisted then abdication would be the only answer. I cannot remember a period in my lifetime when one subject held centre stage for so long. The evening papers had a field day with new headlines on the crisis with each edition. Then on Friday, December 11th, only twelve days after the Bishop of Bradford's sermon, the newsvendors were shouting "King Abdicates". The country was quite stunned and that evening there were few who did not listen to Edward's radio broadcast, which was relayed world-wide. We all heard the King's short message in silence and I remember the remark made by one of my friends, who was almost the same age as Edward, "I always worshipped him. Thank God I didn't turn out like him".

Next morning we learned that the former King had been driven to Portsmouth, where he boarded a destroyer which took him to France. Now that the decision had been made, from being revered, he was reviled by the majority, who could not find a good word to say about the hitherto most popular member of the Royal Family. Such is public opinion.

On the following day, Saturday, we had another proclamation, the second within the year (something of a record in modern times) and George VI became King. Instead of the suave Edward, we now had his brother, who was shy, diffident, stammered badly and had always, whenever possible, avoided the limelight. No wonder the country was shocked by the turn of events, royalty was at its lowest ebb. Looking back, how wrong we all were — it was all for the best. True, the new King had difficulties, but his Queen more than made up for them. As far as Edward was concerned, he quickly forfeited any remaining love that people had for him. His clear admiration for Adolf Hitler and the growing might of Germany destroyed any doubts over the abdication. We were much better off without him as subsequent events proved.

On that eventful day, December 12th, many traders were ruefully viewing memorabilia already purchased in advance of Edward's Coronation. The souvenirs had one thing in common, a portrait of the king who was never crowned. Clearance sales got rid of some of the stuff but many fingers were burned. A friend of mine bought in 1971, thirty five years later, a job lot from a Birmingham source. Included in the assortment were thousands and thousands of Edward VIII lapel badges, which he proceeded to send to the dump. Manufacturers, having lost a great deal of money, now had to set to to provide stock in readiness for the Coronation of George VI. Doubtless they were wise enough to insure against a further cancellation.

Chapter Eleven 1937
Hitler demands living space

In 1936, Gaumont-British purchased the site occupied by Bon Marche and the Angel Hotel in Fisherton Street to accommodate a new super-cinema to replace the Picture House, now usually referred to as a flea-pit. Bon Marche moved to smaller premises quite close by, but closed before the outbreak of the war in 1939. Almost at the same time that Gaumont completed their purchase, Associated British Cinemas announced that they had bought the house and gardens on the corner of Chipper Lane and Endless Street formerly owned by Doctor Kempe. When the news got round that both companies were contemplating cinemas, each with a 1,500-seater capacity, it was thought that one or other would retire from the scene. But no, both went ahead and the building of Associated British Cinemas' Regal provided free entertainment, as citizens gazed at massive steel-work being eased into place by spidermen walking on girders swinging from a massive crane. It was breathtaking to watch these nerveless workmen walking nonchalantly along a twelve-inch wide strip of steel about seventy feet above street level.

ABC got moving rather faster than Gaumont-British, for they were able to open the Regal in February 1937 while the new Picture House was delayed until September. The rush to complete the Regal possibly meant that corners were cut, for the day after the official opening, plaster fell from the ceiling above the circle. Fortunately it was a one-off situation. Neither company could have known at the time just how fortuitous their decision was, for when war came along both cinemas, together with the Gaumont Palace, were packed for almost every performance, no matter what film was shown.

On Easter Saturday, March 27th, Gwen and I were married at

Catherine Street decorated once again — this time to celebrate the Coronation of King George VI and Queen Elizabeth in 1937.

The Regal, at the junction of Endless Street and Chipper Lane, opened during February 1937, showing Shirley Temple in Captain January. The hoarding on the corner was soon to be replaced by Allan R. Snell's tobacconist shop.

Romsey Abbey. That sounds very grand, but the Abbey is the only Church of England in that town and is thus the parish church. We spent the first few months living with relatives, then found rooms in Palmer Road before moving to a bungalow on the Laverstock Hall Estate later in the year. Like most young couples we were hard up, so I worked any available overtime and did all sorts of odd jobs to augment our income.

The big event of the year was the Coronation, held on May 12th. Despite the long trade depression, Salisbury put on an excellent show. Blue Boar Row was especially pleasing, Style and Gerrish making use of their parapet sign, which had extensions for the occasion making it almost a hundred and twenty feet in length. The wording on this, God Save our King and Queen, was written in Trajan Roman lettering, three feet in height. How do I remember? It was the largest sign I had ever produced. Below this, yard-wide fluted red, white and blue bunting was surmounted by golden crowns. The whole display looked truly magnificent. Many other buildings were also beautifully decorated, if not on the same lavish scale. Unfortunately, the weather was not equal to that enjoyed at the Silver Jubilee two years earlier. Neither was it nearly as bad as the deluge at the time of the Seven Hundredth Anniversary in 1927.

Celebrations started on Sunday, May 9th, with the procession of the Mayor and Corporation to the Cathedral, followed by a Beating the Retreat by the Band and Drums of the 2nd Battalion Royal Warwickshire Regiment in Blue Boar Row. Similar ceremonies have taken place there many times since 1937, but I believe this was the first.

On Wednesday the 12th (Coronation Day), there was an early start for the Service of Thanksgiving in the Cathedral. It finished by 10.30am, which allowed people to return home to listen to the broadcast of the Coronation in London, the first occasion that the ceremony had such a world-wide audience. For those not wishing to listen — they were few — entertainment had been laid on in Victoria Park. At two thirty in the afternoon, Salisbury had its usual procession, following the usual route and it was of the usual high standard. By 1937 we were getting used to these mammoth processions — after all, the Coronation one was the fourth in nine years. Little did we know that it would be almost fifteen years before another was possible. Even while the procession was in progress, there were events in Victoria Park. These included a six-a-side football tournament, a bowling competition, a miniature golf championship, and variety performances. The great thing was, everything was FREE!

One competition which proved to be hilarious was organised by St Martin's Men's Club. Competitors had to sing a completed verse of any song, with a small live pig tucked under the arm. I can't imagine a similar event being allowed these days — I expect even back in 1937 there were a few complaints. During the evening we had dancing, followed by one of the finest firework displays ever staged in the city. It lasted for three quarters of an hour, the finale being portraits of the King and Queen. As soon as the display was completed, a torchlight procession and fancy dress parade left the park for the Market Place, where community singing had been organised, the words of songs being shown on a screen erected at the top of the Guildhall. Even this was not the end, dancing followed in Blue Boar Row, led by the Mayor, Major Rawlence DSO, who took as his partner the lady who had just won first prize in the fancy dress parade. The celebrations did not finish until one a.m., when the citizens retired to their beds, very tired and very happy.

Even while the country was en fête we were not allowed to forget the shadow hanging over us. The news of the bombing by German planes of a completely undefended Spanish town, Guernica, horrified us. Using the new screaming dive-bomber technique, the Nazis destroyed the town by high explosive, followed by incendiary bombs. Then such poor inhabitants as were left were subjected to machine gunning. It was the first real warning of the terrors of air-power and they were vividly portrayed by pictures in every paper and the newsreels. Now, we knew what to expect. The number of casualties in Guernica was never known, but the German action left a feeling of horror around the world.

Later that year, Japan followed the German example and gave Shanghai the same treatment. The war between China and Japan was now in its sixth year, but because of the great distance between us and the Far East, was somewhat down-graded or completely forgotten. All this was followed by a meeting in Berlin between the two dictators Hitler and Mussolini, when they both demanded colonies to provide their countries with so-called "living space". "Musso", as he was tagged, talked of the resurrection of the Roman Empire, Adolf talked of expansion to the East. At about the same time, details began to be published of a new concentration camp — Buchenwald — a name to become notorious. We all carried on with our work, well aware of the inevitability of another World War.

During that year of 1937, I first came into contact with family illness resulting in hospital treatment. Early on, just prior to my wedding, Aunt Gertrude, whom I had always looked upon as a second mum, went into the Infirmary for a serious operation, a colostomy. She was forced to give up work at only fifty eight years of age and spent the next ten years as an invalid. She w̃ lovely lady.

Gwen and I had only been married for three months when she too became ill, while on a visit to her mother at Romsey. I was sent for and arrived in the nick of time to accompany her in the ambulance which took her to the Royal South Hants Hospital in Southampton. Appendicitis had been diagnosed, but there was so much inflammation that the doctors decided not to operate. She spent the next fortnight in a bed propped up at a twenty degree angle, which allowed the poison to drain away. When discharged, she was still very poorly and was told that as soon as the appendix became painful again she was to contact the Infirmary, when the operation would be immediately performed.

It was not a good year for us, as there were problems in respect of the bungalows being built on the Laverstock Hall Estate. The builder's brochure, which had been printed early in the year, stated that each property would have mains water and sewerage, electricity and gas. It also said that the rates for a two-bedroomed detached bungalow would be about two shillings and sixpence per week. At that time only the contract for gas installation had been signed and negotiations for the electricity supply were in their infancy. But the real problem arose because the estate was in the Salisbury and Wilton District Council area and they possessed no facilities for mains water or sewage disposal. By early summer, some thirty properties had been sold and the delay meant the builders were not very popular. We were given various excuses, but it took until October before an agreement was thrashed out. Salisbury City Council agreed to supply the District Council with water and also connect up the sewerage system. The District Council would then sign a contract with the builder, who would then offer the facilities to householders. Had the estate not been just those two hundred yards outside the city boundary the supply would not have had to go through so many hands. The District Council only added a very small percentage to the bill they received from the city but the whole mess-up was to lead to real problems when we got our first accounts from the builders in 1939.

Through this delay, we were up against it as regards temporary living accommodation, but eventually managed to rent a couple of rooms in a four-storey house off the Devizes Road. Our sitting room was on the ground floor and the bedroom on the third, while the cooking facilities, which we shared with the landlord, were in the basement. This cost us ten shillings a week.

We had only been there a few weeks when Gwen spent another fortnight in hospital while she had her appendix removed. I used to visit each evening between six thirty and seven pm, but one Monday I was delayed and only arrived a few minutes before turning out time. I was just leaving off work at Brown Street when I heard the sound of a fire engine, which stopped not far away. Then there was the sound of another and then a third. Someone was shouting "It's the Co-op in Milford Street", so off I dashed. When I reached the Co-operative Society's furniture department, the firemen were busily engaged in the store looking for staff. This went on for about ten minutes, during which time the fire was getting a real hold and then it was found the staff were gathered in the street watching operations. By this time the fire was well advanced and we gazed as the Volunteer Fire Brigade did their best to bring the flames under control. They did a wonderful job, although heat was intense, I remember watching the large plate glass window change colour — eventually becoming a yellow-green before collapsing. A fireman friend of mine, with a colleague, was playing water on the building from the roof of the adjoining Cathedral Hotel. There was a sudden shout of "Look out, Cecil, that wall's cracking," and we could indeed see the fissure appearing in the hotel's wall. My friend and his mate made a mad dash across the roof for safety and fell through a skylight, fortunately with little physical damage. Fortunate indeed, for Cecil was no eight-stone weakling, he was a fifteen-stone strong man. At about ten minutes to seven, the fire was under control and I remembered that I had to be at the Infirmary by seven. I made it by the skin of my teeth.

During August and September, I was working quite long hours for the new Picture House was opening on September 27th. It was a truly luxurious theatre when compared with the old flea-pit. The entrance hall and foyer seemed the size of a football pitch, with loads of space for the display of the publicity which we were to supply weekly. The feature film shown during the opening week was *King Solomon's Mines,* starring Paul Robeson. It was billed as being based on Rider Haggard's great book, which had been a favourite of mine when at St Martin's Boys' School, but any resemblance was purely coincidental.

That fire at the Co-op was to have a happy sequel for me a salvage sale was held in the Three Swans Yard in late November. I went along to see what was on offer. Most of the lots were fire-damaged, but at the back of a trestle table I saw three pieces of folding wooden trellis and, although one piece was badly damaged, decided to bid. It was knocked down to me for three shillings and sixpence. I thought it was indeed a bargain. After completion of the sale, I went to the clerk and paid, then made my way to collect the trellis. I gave my ticket to the porter who said "Have you got some trucks?" I looked at him and replied: "What, to carry three pieces of trellis?" The porter said: "There's all this too, you know," and pointed not only under that table but to the ones on either side. For three shillings and sixpence I had bought the Co-op's complete stock, I went and got some hand trucks, then, with the aid of a friend, started pushing my bargain to Laverstock — it took three journeys. I was able to fix trellis all round and across the garden. It was in all heights from two feet to six feet and a number of my new neighbours were only too pleased to buy from me at a reduced rate. The cost to me for each section was just over a halfpenny — a bargain indeed.

*The New Picture House opened in September
1937. During the early Fifties it became the
Odeon and in 1962 was purchased at a bargain
price to become the City Hall.*

*The disastrous fire at the Salisbury Co-operative Society's furnishing
department on the corner of Queen Street and Milford Street in
September 1937. The blaze was as fierce as anything seen in the city
during the century.*

We had moved into the new bungalow in early November, waiting until electricity had been connected, though some of our more anxious neighbours made the step a week or two earlier and had to manage with oil lamps and candles. For several weeks there was a problem, until fences were erected by the contractor, for we had a three-month-old puppy, a tiny spaniel called Peggy. The garden was just a builder's tip, full of whole bricks, half bricks, quarter bricks, and pieces of batten. It took ages to clear up. Then, when I started digging, I came across great lumps of concrete that had been buried just below the surface.

Shortly after we moved in the weather turned very cold and the electricity supply was off for five days, but it was pleasant just sitting by the light of a wood fire. Most of us on the estate burned wood that winter — there was loads of it to be had for free as a timber merchant had purchased the woods which were part of the park and only bothered to remove the tree trunks, so we used to spend each weekend collecting all the quite sizeable branches.

I remember that we went to my wife's home for a couple of days at Christmas and arrived back to find the water pipes were frozen. We really were a couple of rookies not to drain the system when temperatures were well below zero. There is no teacher to beat experience.

Chapter Twelve 1938
Peace in our time

Early in the New Year, I was given a quantity of old Portland stone by the estate builder. This consisted of about ten blocks measuring some two feet on each side and with these I set to making the front patch into a rock garden with a small pond. The first job was transporting the stone from the old Laverstock Hall, half a mile away. I took one look and decided the blocks were almost immovable until broken into pieces. I borrowed a seven-pound sledge hammer from Dad and started banging away without making any impression. It was then that I realised that stone, like wood, has a grain, and that when it was hit on the correct side it would split quite easily. There was a nasty fright for me while I was doing this job as a couple of adders slithered out, highly indignant at having their home disturbed. In a hurry, as I've always been, and to the amusement of my neighbours, I fixed up a floodlight in the garden so that I was able to carry on the placing of stones during the dark winter evenings.

During March, war seemed even closer when on the 14th Hitler annexed Austria. Many years later, in 1966, I did business with, and then became good friends with, one of the victims of this aggression. R--- W---- was a seventeen-year-old Viennese Jew, in his last year at school before entering university. He had gone to lessons as usual on that fateful Monday morning and then learned of the invasion. When the lunch break came, R--- was met by a family servant, who told him that his father had been arrested. The possibility of a German coup had been discussed and a decision taken that should such an event happen, the family would move into Czechoslovakia to an uncle. So R---, instead of going home to lunch, made his way to Prague, the only one of his family to succeed in escaping. He stayed there until the following January, when he moved into Poland, from there a Jewish escape committee brought him in July to this country. The following year he was for a few months interned on the Isle of Man, but was later released to spend the rest of the war on essential work in Lancashire. When he finally went back to his native country, he discovered that he only had one relative left in the world — an eighty-year-old uncle in Budapest. All the others had vanished into concentration camps.

R—— became a successful businessman who always feared another invasion, possibly Russian. With this in mind, he salted money away in bank accounts in several countries so that an avenue of escape might always be open to him and his family.

While all this was happening, closer to home Mr Gething was busy on his lifelong ambition, to stage a revue. He had always dabbled with the stage and was a popular performer at local shows over a wide area, now he was preparing an attraction that would be staged at the Victoria Hall and last for a week, from Easter Monday through to the following Saturday. For an amateur production *Nightlights* really was excellent. Mr Gething wrote most of the sketches and gathered together some wonderful local talent — the only professional act was a lady conjuror (whose fee was an astronomical thirteen pounds — a lot of money in 1938).

The eight girls who formed a professional looking dancing troupe were well trained by Mrs Lil Spackman, the wife of the former stage manager at the Palace Theatre. At this time she had become more than plump and it was very difficult to visualise the lady as she must have been thirty years before when one of the famous Tiller girls. As a result of this successful show, a handsome donation went to the Infirmary.

On the Thursday after Easter, my wife went to see her doctor, who confirmed her pregnancy, so we looked forward to our first child arriving in October.

That summer can be summed up in three words: work, work, work. Every penny counted. In addition to my job, I was trying to transform the builder's dump into a worthwhile garden and had also taken on an allotment about 100 yards from my home. This was really hard going, for at one time it had been a refuse tip, then a poultry farm. It was the chicken manure that laid the golden egg, for the potatoes I planted were so successful that Dad, a lifelong gardener, said that he'd never seen anything like it. One root had a total of thirty one potatoes, which turned the scales at over twelve pounds. Unfortunately, during the following winter the owner sold the ground, so all my endeavours went to naught.

The test matches that year, against the Australians, were for England a vast improvement on 1934. We had a number of young and talented new boys, but no-one could have guessed what they would give us during the final test at the Oval in August. Len Hutton, a twenty-one-year old Yorkshireman, broke the record when he ran up a massive three hundred and sixty four. He was helped by centuries from Leyland and Hardstaff — the England side declaring at the unbelievable total of nine hundred and three for seven. They had so tired and demoralised the Aussies that when it was their turn to bat they were twice dismissed cheaply, so that at last we got our own back for the big scores they had amassed both in 1930 and '34. England won by an innings and five hundred and seventy nine runs.

Hardly was the test match out of the way than it was back to the European situation. Full of confidence, after his annexation of Austria, when hardly an official word of dissent had been heard from Britain, France or Russia, Hitler felt it was time for his next move, so he looked east at Czechoslovakia. His moves always took a familiar pattern — first he would plant trained agitators among the German minority in the country of his choice. In no time, the world would be made aware of the suffering which that country's Government were inflicting on Hitler's compatriots. Then pressure would be applied for self-government, quickly followed by demands for union with the Fatherland.

Prior to late August of 1938, few people in this country even knew of the existence of Sudetenland. Through September, it became the main topic of conversation. In the middle of the month, Sudetan Germans broke off talks with the Czech Government and martial law was declared. This country, in co-operation with France, produced a plan under which Sudetanland would be ceded to Germany. The Czechs disagreed and ordered general mobilisation. In an effort for peace our Prime Minister flew to Germany, cap in hand, but without success. Hitler gave him the cold shoulder.

As war looked increasingly imminent, emergency preparations

were put in hand. A loud-speaker van toured Salisbury asking for volunteers willing to dig trenches in the Greencroft. The response was amazing, for hundreds turned up, my father and I among them. The ground had been pegged out with markers indicating the proposed zig-zag trenches, following the design which had proved so effective in the First World War. Each section was ten feet in length, four feet in width and seven feet deep — Dad and I dug a section on each of the first three evenings, before I retired with badly blistered hands, like many others that week. This was my introduction to pick and shovel work.

There was a rush of recruits wishing to join the armed forces and the tension built each day, until on Wednesday, September 28th, just as we were expecting Germany to invade Czechoslovakia, Hitler called a four-power conference in Munich. Our Prime Minister, Mr Neville Chamberlain, flew out to meet the other heads of state — Daladier of France, Mussolini of Italy and, of course, Hitler himself. They hammered out an agreement, without Czech approval, ceding Sudetenland, with its German minority, to the Fatherland.

Digging trenches in the Greencroft during the Munich crisis of September 1938. The author's father (second from left) is seen with three young workmates from Edwards Bros. On the left is Ginger Edwards, a grandson of the firm's founder.

On his return, on the Friday, Chamberlain was greeted as the peacemaker. He waved a piece of paper as he descended the steps from the plane, the document signed by both Hitler and himself would, he said, ensure peace in our time and was peace with honour. He went on to the House of Commons where he was given a rapturous reception. The odd man out, whose scowling features were portrayed next day in most of the national papers, was Winston Churchill. Whether Mr Chamberlain genuinely believed in his own words is a moot point, as rearmament in this country went on apace. The year of peace that he gained was to prove all important for, without it, our air defences that won the Battle of Britain in 1940 would not have materialised. During the week following the infamous Munich agreement, those who had volunteered for military service during the crisis were allowed to recant if they wished.

I remember that on the following Monday, my wife and I paid a visit to the Gaumont Palace to see Walt Disney's wonderful film *Snow White and the Seven Dwarfs*. Although I have possibly seen it on three occasions since that time, it is still for me a masterpiece.

Wednesday, October 12th, 1938 is a day I shall never forget. At about six in the morning, my wife told me to go and ring the midwife, who, after close questioning, said she would cycle over from her Bemerton home, some three miles away, at about ten o'clock. I asked if that was soon enough and got the reply "It will be hours yet". During the day my mother and aunt arrived. Later, after tea, my sister. The midwife had been right, she'd seen it all many times, for it was ten minutes to nine in the evening before my son, Gordon, announced his arrival in the world with a loud cry. I had forecast correctly because the wooden crib which I made (decorated with Disney figures) was painted pale blue. (Strangely when my daughter was born five years later, I had repainted it pink — second sight?)

When my son was six weeks old, it was discovered that he was less than his birth weight, so a spell in hospital resulted. The doctors and nurses tried various foods and after some five weeks hit on one that suited him. Thanks to Cow and Gate, by the time he reached six months he looked a bonny child.

Chapter Thirteen 1939
Peace flies out of the window

In January, a chicken came home to roost when the residents of the Laverstock Hall Estate received a nasty shock one morning. The postman arrived with a sizeable bill of between five and eight pounds for each householder. These accounts from the estate builder were in respect of water and sewerage charges and meant that rates were now at least double those quoted in his 1937 brochure.

During the next few days, we talked of little else. The five to seven pounds of 1939 would be approximately £250 to £350 by 1991 levels. It was a lot of money. Within a week, several of us got together and called a public meeting in the village hall. This was addressed by Mr Allan B. Lemon, the Salisbury solicitor, renowned as a fighter for public causes. He was quite a character, not much above five feet in height, constantly peering over his spectacles and a dynamic speaker.

The tiny village hall was crammed full — we were jammed in so tightly, it was like a football crowd at a cup tie. Mr Lemon outlined the case and thought that we had all been misled, though not intentionally. He suggested that we formed an association and all signed a document bearing responsibility for our share of any legal costs. He would then seek Counsel's opinion on our behalf. After this he invited questions and many of those responding showed anger at the charges. One gentleman suggested that no-one paid the account, which led to someone else saying this would lead to water supplies being cut off. At this a rather frightened lady asked if water could be cut off to a house where young children lived. The subject was well aired before Mr Lemon departed back to Salisbury by taxi.

After his departure we got down to business. The Laverstock Hall

Estate Ratepayers' Association was formed, we all put our names to a hastily prepared document agreeing to share legal costs, and a chairman and committee were elected. I agreed to act as secretary.

During the next month there were several consultations with Mr Lemon, who kindly agreed to meet us in the evenings. The relevant details were sent off to Counsel and we eagerly awaited his opinion. It arrived one evening with a note from our solicitor asking to be excused from attending the meeting owing to a heavy cold. I therefore had the job of reading the six closely typed sheets to the assembled committee. When I had completed the task, someone said "What does it all mean". The chairman and I pointed out that Counsel thought that the builder was covered by the word "approximately" when calculating the possible charge for rates printed on the brochure, so our case was not strong. The news shook several members who had been quite vociferous, they collapsed rather like pricked balloons and were ready to listen to reason. I suggested that we kept the opinion secret and, through Mr Lemon, tried to reach a compromise solution with the builder.

The chairman and I were appointed to act on the committee's behalf and from then on it became rather like a game of poker. We had several joint meetings with the builder and his solicitor and within six weeks a solution was hammered out, one which was far better than we had a right to expect. The builder's profit margin which he was allowed to add to the Council's bill for water and sewage disposal was fixed at only five per cent to cover all his work in the matter, rendering half-yearly accounts with the collection of debts. He also agreed to a Committee of Inspection, appointed by the Association, examining his books prior to accounts being sent out. We called another meeting of all members and, after the committee had been thoroughly slated, it was agreed to accept the proposal. I remember the remarks directed at me: "Whose side are you on?" After the meeting one member even suggested that the builder might have made it worth my while! So much for trying to help. The agreement and the Inspection Committee worked well and saved the ratepayers money over succeeding years. It was my first taste of public work. One that taught me you cannot please everyone.

By this time, thanks possibly to the money that rearmament was bringing to the economy, trade was increasing. A Home and Fashions Exhibition, sponsored by Salisbury Chamber of Commerce, was held in the Victoria Hall in March 1939 and lasted for eight days. This was quite successful and brought us a great deal of display work, not only for the local exhibition but also for others run by the organisers in various locations. I recall that the very welcome overtime payments paid for a hall carpet.

In the middle of March, Hitler recommenced his ranting and raving, demanding more of Czechoslovakia. True to form, the German newspapers reported that the treatment of Germans and Slovaks by the Czechs was intolerable. This was the prelude to the invasion and annexation of the rest of that country by Hitler's forces on March 15th. A fortnight later, Britain and France gave Poland guarantees of help against attack.

The same week, a recruiting drive for air raid precaution organisations was held in Salisbury. The response was tremendous. I volunteered for the Auxiliary Fire Service, heard nothing for weeks, attended four lectures on poison gas and then, in common with thirty-odd class mates, was told my services were not required as there had been over-enrollment.

Unemployment in the city was by this time drastically reduced through the number of new Army camps being built in the area, plus the vast RAF munitions depot in the old Chilmark Quarries and the Naval arms depot at Dean Hill. Far higher wages were paid to those working on these projects than could be earned in the city and many left regular employment to make money while they could — after all, what did it matter if war was coming. I remember one gentleman, an assistant in a high class tailors, increased his wages by over fifty per cent by becoming a painter's labourer.

Despite the apparent inevitability of war, Goddards went into a fair-sized expansion when, after purchasing the premises of several small businesses on the north side of Winchester Street, they had a magnificent car showroom built. Unfortunately, hardly had they moved cars in than the premises were requisitioned for war work.

Easter of that year was rather ruined by the news. On Good Friday, Mussolini decided it was time to get in on the act, grab some more of the so-called living space, and invade Albania. King

Zog fled and we warned the Italians that no further aggression would be tolerated, guarantees being given to both Greece and Romania. Next, following the usual noises from Hitler, the Dutch troops were ordered to the German border, bringing forth more guarantees from Britain and France, this time to Holland, Denmark and Switzerland. We were handing them out like confetti.

All this was followed, on April 27th, by the Government bringing in the first ever peacetime Act of Conscription. The following month, all males between the ages of twenty and twenty one had to register, with a view to spending six months in the Forces prior to being transferred to the Territorial Army. As events turned out, the six months were to become more than six years for most of the conscripts, who received pay of ten shillings and sixpence each week.

There was one bright spot at this time. Portsmouth reached the FA Cup Final at Wembley. Almost everyone living in the Southern Counties was right behind them, even though they were ranked as complete outsiders by the betting fraternity. Their opponents, Wolverhampton Wanderers, were a good young side, managed by the ebullient Major Buckley, whom the media claimed was giving his team glandular injections. As I had to work on that Saturday afternoon, I hired a radio and so was able to hear the commentary (the last for seven years). Far from being overwhelmed by their clever opponents, Portsmouth shocked everyone by going three goals up in the first half hour. Wolves then pulled one back and the half time score was 3-1. During the interval, the commentators gave the impression that Wolves were coming back and the second half could well be different. To prove them wrong, just after the start of the second half Portsmouth scored a fourth goal and then proceeded to contain their opponents, running out easy winners by four goals to one.

A few days later, in a radio speech, Hitler offered Denmark a non-aggression pact. Then, in late May, while Russia, France and Britain were contemplating an alliance, the German Chancellor, with more ranting and raving, made known his desire to annexe the Baltic port of Danzig at the north of the Polish Corridor. Once again, Germany was warned that further aggression would mean war.

During June, the country was absorbed in news close to home when the submarine *Thetis* sank in Liverpool Bay with more than seventy men on board. The rescue attempts were vividly reported over three days by newspapers and radio and although seven men were saved, the submarine, which had been hauled to the surface, sank again when hawsers snapped.

In early August, when my employer told me that he was contemplating closing the business and taking a job which had been offered him, I asked if I could buy it and run it on my own. As he expressed his agreement, I talked the matter over with my wife and decided to take a chance. He then started work on a job a short distance away from the city and I carried on running the business for him until the legal side could be completed. I had little spare cash, but thought the weekly contracts to supply publicity to four Gaumont-British Cinemas would be sufficient to provide a solid basis for a one-man band. I moved to two very small rooms on the opposite side of Brown Street, on the first floor over the office of the National Deposit Friendly Society. The total area was only 150 square feet. The rent of six shillings now seems quite ludicrous, but I realised that in the early days it was essential to keep overheads to a minimum. Heating was by means of a portable gas fire, given me by my sister. It had cost her five shillings and elevenpence at Timothy Whites. My father, always ready to help, made up a bench in situ. It measured only eight feet by three feet six inches, but a great deal of work was produced on it during the next few years.

The premises were a part of what had been the Black Horse inn, which until the advent of the railways was one of Salisbury's large coaching hotels. I remember, on the first occasion that I was working late in the evening, I was sitting quietly at the bench when I heard a scratching down by my feet and a rat suddenly dashed across the room to an alcove in the opposite corner and dived down a hole. He was followed by two others. Next morning, I got some sheet metal and blocked up the hole, which stopped the vermin bothering me during the next few weeks. Then they gnawed a new hole in the skirting board by the side of the metal, so once again I blocked the hole. This went on until almost all the skirting on that side of the room was covered by sheet tin. It was no wonder that I had the problem for, without doubt, the rats' ancestors had made the same one-way journey for many, many years and now they had food on either side, for one neighbour was a potato merchant, the other ran a fish and chip shop.

In the attic above my rooms, covered in dust, were the files of a solicitor who had occupied the premises many years before. I think it possible that Mr Sanger, the man in question, had been called up for military service in 1916 (the date of the last letters) and had stored the papers in the loft, intending to resume his practice on his return. But he never came back. It was a sad little piece of history. Opposite were Tom Singleton's premises. He ran S.T.B. Motors, was a first class engineer and dealt in secondhand cars. When I moved in, Tom told me one day not to stay there too long because the roof would fall in. True, the tiled roof of the very old building was all shapes, but I visited the premises in 1990, some fifty one years after Tom's comment, and it still looked the same. At that time, work was being carried out on the ground floor and when matchboard wainscot and the plaster was removed, the method of the building's construction was revealed. There appeared to be no foundations as we know today, just massive blocks of limestone supporting the brickwork. I wonder when that stone was first put into place.

Each day, as August progressed, war seemed ever nearer. We wondered if there would be a last-minute reprieve like the one of the previous year. There was one bright spot on the horizon. It seemed that Britain and France were about to sign an alliance with Russia and we felt that surely even Hitler would never be foolish enough to take on the might of the three countries — one to the east and two to the west. Then, on the 17th, Germany closed its borders with Poland. Three days later Polish troops were rushed to the area and Britain and France once again pledged their support. In this country, reservists were called to the colours, but suddenly, on the 23rd, the morning papers told us that the unbelievable had happened. Instead of the expected triangular alliance between Britain, France and Russia, the latter had now signed a non-aggression pact with Hitler. We were all shell-shocked. Over the next week the situation deteriorated day by day. Germany sent Poland an ultimatum on the return of Danzig and the Polish

Corridor. Children were evacuated from the large cities in both Britain and France. Salisbury provided shelter for many sent out of Portsmouth, the WVS doing a splendid job from their newly acquired office, a former high class shoe shop on Blue Boar Row. Normal work seemed an irrelevance for it was difficult to concentrate.

However, on the evening of Wednesday, August 30th, most Salisbury men put war preparations to one side for a couple of hours relaxation, watching Salisbury Corinthians play Arsenal (yes, THE Arsenal) at Victoria Park. This unusual match was arranged as a thank you to the Corries, for their opponents had just signed the outstanding young goalkeeper George Marks from the home team. George went on to play for England in several wartime Internationals. I went to the match with a friend, Doug White, a chemist who worked at Porton. We walked from Laverstock and as we went down Moberly Road, sandbags were being filled to protect an ARP post. The crowd on that lovely warm August evening was the largest I've ever seen at the Park. We saw a most entertaining game and were impressed by the team of Arsenal youngsters, who won by three goals to nil. All the way home our conversation centred on the forthcoming conflict, the question was not "Will war break out?" — it was "When?".

We went to work as usual on Friday, September 1st. Then, at about half past nine, Tom Singleton, who kept his radio going full blast all the time he was working, was in the street shouting that the Germans had invaded Poland. From then on for the rest of the day little groups gathered everywhere. People were asking "Where do we go from here?" What could Britain and France do to help the Polish? We were too far away to send planes, it was too dangerous for the Navy to enter the Baltic and it was generally felt that the guarantees we had given were worthless. Although there had been talk of another war for many years (I remember the Smyrna scare when the Turks invaded Greece in 1922), now it was upon us. It was still a shock. It was an overcast and cold day or was it our mood. Everyone listened to the radio expecting a declaration of war at any moment. Some thought air raids would start without a formal declaration and stupid rumours began their rounds, but we reached the end of the day and nothing seemed to have happened.

Saturday, September 2nd was a most peculiar day. The whole country appeared to be at a standstill. Again, I remember it as a day when the sun seemed to be blotted out. I completed, after a struggle, the publicity material for the new Picture House and delivered it late in the afternoon, to be told by the manager, George Howes, that in the event of hostilities all places of entertainment would be closed. He was in the process of making arrangements to live on the premises (this was an order from head office) and had just purchased a camp bed.

Few people patronised the cinema that day and no-one had time to be interested in football results. This was a pity as the afternoon's games produced some peculiar scores. Even staid Bournemouth had run up their all-time record and trounced Northampton by ten goals to nil. I wonder if they were playing against a team of young boys and old men, for the call-up of all reservists during the previous weeks must have had a profound effect. We did not realise that those games would be the last League football for seven whole seasons. Many a promising career must have been ruined, for seven years is a long time in a professional footballer's life.

The news that all cinemas were to be closed was a body blow to me, for I was now committed to taking on the business and my mainstay would be gone. My wife and I spent the evening trying to think of a solution without success. By bedtime there was still no news of any reaction to Hitler's invasion of Poland. It was a most unreal situation.

In contrast to the previous two days, Sunday dawned brightly, it was much warmer and I got ready to finish painting my bungalow. While we were having breakfast, the BBC announced that the Prime Minister would broadcast to the nation at 11.15am. Although I started painting the front door, the work was done with the greatest of difficulty as my friends kept coming to discuss the situation. By eleven o'clock quite a small crowd had gathered, but it broke up just afterwards when we went to listen to what Mr Chamberlain had to say. The Prime Minister sounded a sad and disillusioned man. It was less than a year since his return from Munich, waving the piece of paper saying that Britain and Germany would never go to war again. Now he had to tell the country that no reply had been received in response to the ultimatum sent to Hitler by France and Britain and so, from eleven o'clock that morning, a state of war existed. I went outside with the intention of finishing the front door. I needn't have bothered, for a passing friend called me to the gate to mull over the news. In a few minutes there were probably half a dozen of us chatting away, when suddenly an army lorry swept round the corner, driven by another friend, a reservist, who had been called up about a week earlier. He slowed down and shouted "Can't stop — I've broken convoy. Just off to Southampton — off to France, must say goodbye to the Missus". He sped on down the road and round the corner to his bungalow in Beechcroft Road. Within a couple of minutes he was back. The lorry screeched to a halt and he jumped down, pumped each one of us by the hand, with "Cheerio, old chap", jumped back in, started off and sped round the corner. We watched him go in silence, suddenly the war was real. Later that day, the poor chap was back, having returned from Southampton after dropping equipment, and he now had a sleeping-out pass. I remember this false alarm as the one funny thing that happened on that day.

That afternoon, I was offered a writing job at the almost completed Army camp at Winterbourne Gunner and accepted, as it would help me over the immediate future. Somewhat heartened by this good news, I set to with a will to make blackout screens. These were constructed from one inch by quarter-inch wooden laths with three-ply joints and covered in blackout paper. Although light in weight, they must have been strong, for they lasted until restrictions were lifted in 1944. In common with most people, my wife was busy sticking gummed brown paper tape on all windows, until they took on the appearance of leaded lights. This was supposed to guard against the splintering of glass in the event of the inevitable blast from bombing.

During early evening, I had to go into Salisbury and remember self consciously carrying my gas mask in its cardboard box, suspended from my shoulder by a piece of string. I think most people felt the same. The blackout was a severe blow for Salisbury, as the city's new and bang up-to-date electric street lighting had only been switched on during the previous week. It had replaced the Victorian gas lamp standards and now was to remain switched off for the next five years. On the BBC that evening we learned that the sirens had sounded in London for the first time, that broadcasting would now be much restricted and that announcers would always preface reading the news by giving their names, so that people could recognise their voices in case the enemy started fake broadcasts to cause alarm.

I went off to Winterbourne Camp by cycle the following morning, armed with my kit. (It was a glorious day compared with the previous Friday and Saturday). The rest of that week was spent writing names on doors in plain block lettering. All the huts were uniform size, sixty feet by twenty, of corrugated iron with matchboard lining. The week gave me an insight into the problems that arise when a large body of men from many different backgrounds are thrust into each other's company. When the siren sounded for meal breaks they were almost like animals in their rush to be served in the canteen, even jumping on to and over tables in their haste to be fed. I used to sit and eat my sandwiches quietly and then when they were finished would carry on with my sign-writing.

That was the pattern until the Wednesday, when I was threatened by a self-appointed shop steward, who told me in no uncertain fashion that if I valued my health I would not work during meal breaks. I remember his words "Nobody works on this camp, unless we say so. When the siren goes, you stop and don't start until it blows again". I also remember a row one evening, when a gang of painters started washing their hands just prior to the five minutes agreed for the task. The foreman remonstrated and bawled out the charge hand, who then turned, egged on by colleagues and thinking his men would back him, to ridicule the other's knowledge of his trade. He was quickly told that he was no longer a charge hand and when he looked to his gang for support in his accusations, found that most of them had melted away.

One afternoon, someone started a rumour that Hendon had been bombed. It spread like wildfire and some men from that area of London dashed to catch the next train home. Shortly after this, posters were displayed all over the country, stating the penalties faced for spreading false rumours. That week was quite an experience for me, one that on the whole I enjoyed even though I was arriving home, dog tired after a twelve hour day with a six-mile cycle ride, morning and night thrown in.

On Friday, September 8th, it was announced that cinemas were to reopen and I had urgent messages asking me to go along and alter all the dates on publicity showing forthcoming films. I finished my writing at Winterbourne on the Monday and then was able to settle down to business in earnest. I gave up time each day to call on my former employer's regular customers and met with the same remark on many occasions. "What a time to take over a business."

On the war front, although the expected air raids did not happen, there were a few shocks. The liner *Athenia* was torpedoed, as were the battleship *Royal Oak* and aircraft carrier *Courageous*, all with great loss of life.

One of the first wartime jobs that came my way was marking arm bands and haversacks for the thirty trench stewards whose job it was to keep order in the Greencroft shelters. These trenches, dug by voluntary labour almost a year earlier during the Munich crisis, had in the intervening months been lined with pre-cast concrete slabs and fitted with seats and electric lighting that was far from bright. Most of the trench stewards were older people, prepared to do their bit, but no match for some of the courting couples who began to make use of the convenient facilities. To combat this problem the trenches were fitted with doors, opened only when an air raid warning had been sounded.

We soon got used to finding our way around in the blackout with torches, masked so that the lighted aperture was only the size of the old halfpenny. It was also necessary to be on the lookout for road vehicles with headlights masked by grills which prevented light being seen from above. Few people, especially the elderly, went out after dark unless the journey was really necessary. There were those ready to exploit their fellow citizens — numerous so-called luminous devices appeared on the market, guaranteed to shine in the gloom. Most of them were useless but door-to-door salesmen had a field day for a few weeks. Traders soon closed their shops at six o'clock, finding that little trade was being done after dark — one reason being that with the tight blackout regulations it was difficult to tell if a shop was open. At first no "open" signs could be illuminated, but after a few weeks the authorities relaxed and dimly lit ones were allowed. Even buses were blacked out and the interior lighting drastically reduced. One of the worst problems was going from a normally lit building into the black-out. It was several minutes before your eyes became used to the darkness.

In about the second week of the war, I left the Catherine Street entrance of the Gaumont cinema, stupidly did not pause to become accustomed to the gloom and walked slap-bang into the sharp edge of one of the new electric street lighting standards. The blow to my forehead almost knocked me out and when I put my hand to my head I felt blood. I went back into the cinema where they quickly dressed the cut that was some two inches long in the centre of a rapidly rising bump the size of an egg. Most people had similar experiences with the result that everyone took great care.

Before long, premises all over the city were requisitioned for military use, the old Picture House became a recruiting centre, the RSM there being the former head commissionaire from the Gaumont Palace. He was now completely in his element. The Barnard's Cross section of the Teacher Training College became Pay Corps offices and the RASC could be found in several houses in Bourne Avenue. With the influx of so many extra service personnel queues became a regular thing at all three cinemas, dances were held almost nightly at the Assembly Rooms, Cadena Cafe Ballroom and at the Wilton Road Ballroom. One enterprising garage owner at Amesbury who had been having a large new showroom built when war broke out, had it altered to provide a first class ballroom that quickly became popular. Surrounded as it was by troops he could hardly go wrong and soon possessed his own band, the Melville Christie Dance Orchestra, which could be heard regularly on the popular radio feature Workers' Playtime. The nightly dances were always a sell-out. It mattered not that the ballroom resembled a barracks — it provided much needed entertainment, for in addition to dancing, boxing and variety shows attracted the crowds.

The first seven months of the war have always been referred to as the phoney war. Whoever thought up the phrase was somewhat of a genius, because it was so perfectly descriptive. The expected blitzkrieg was conspicuous by its absence — life seemed to go along with few of the problems anticipated. The black-out was the bane of everyone's life, for the restrictions were rigidly enforced by ARP street wardens, whose cry of "Put that light out" was constantly heard. The police force, now some four times its pre-war strength, having been augmented by the addition of full-time police war reservists and part-time special constables, was especially vigilant in the matter of the black-out and many prosecutions of hitherto law-abiding citizens resulted.

My father had been a Special for some months prior to the declaration of war and noticed recurring chinks of light emanating from a certain house, whose occupants had been well known to him for many years. After warning them on two occasions he was obliged to make a report and prosecution followed. My father spent the days prior to his first appearance as a prosecution witness at the city's Petty Sessions in a state of nervous anticipation. The case was all over in a few minutes and the householder fined, but neither he or his wife spoke to Dad thereafter. That first winter the advent of the full moon was a wonderful bonus, for its light enabled us to walk about outside with some freedom, whereas a year later it was usually a herald for a heavy bombing raid.

All this time, armed forces were being drafted to France and the newsreels were filled with pictures of the wonderful Maginot Line, the impregnable defence which France had built along her eastern front bordering Germany. It really would have been a wonderful achievement had it extended to the Channel coast, for it had underground railways and sleeping quarters that looked more like a two star hotel. In September, men aged twenty one were required to register for military service and those in the Salisbury area were quickly called to the Hale Hall in Bedwin Street for medical examination. Any passed as fit usually had call-up papers within a few weeks.

Hitler's answer to the Maginot Line had been his own Ziegfried Line, pooh-poohed by the press in this country as being shoddily erected with constant cracks appearing in the hastily prepared concrete. The popular song of that winter was "We're going to hang out the washing on the Ziegfried Line — have you any dirty washing Mother dear?". I even had an order for a sixteen-sheet poster from Mr Schofield of the Salisbury Steam Laundry which portrayed washing strung along the top of a decrepit fortress and the wording "Don't hang the washing on the Ziegfried Line — just send it to Salisbury Steam Laundry". The events of the next year left egg on the faces of many wiseacres responsible for such twaddle.

In December, about a fortnight before Christmas, we were all heartened at the outcome of the Battle of the River Plate, when the British Cruisers *Exeter, Ajax* and *Achilles,* after an engagement with the German battleship *Admiral Graf Spee* in the Southern Atlantic, forced her to take shelter in a Uruguayan port where she stayed for several days. When the crippled German vessel eventually came out, it was with a skeleton crew who scuttled her — a scene that was well documented by the Americans and shown on newsreels in this country. Salisbury was especially proud that two local men took part in the battle and also in the parade to London's Guildhall when the ships returned. As Winston Churchill, who had resumed his old job as First Lord of the Admiralty on September 3rd, said with his usual brilliant turn of phrase "It warmed the cockles of British hearts".

The difficulty experienced by many people unable to go out as usual because of the blackout began to have a spin-off. Many now became radio addicts and catch-phrases from popular shows became the order of the day. Jack Warner, the star of Garrison Theatre, is remembered for "Mind my bike", the letters he received from "my bruvver Sid" and "Not blue pencil likely". There was also *Monday Night at Eight o'clock* with its signature tune:

> It's Monday Night at Eight o'clock,
> Oh, can't you hear the chimes;
> They're telling you to take an easy chair,
> To settle by the fireside,
> Look at your Radio Times,
> For Monday Night at Eight is on the air.

Without doubt, the most popular show was *It's that Man Again*, shortened by the wartime craze for initials to *ITMA*. Many of the stars from this show made their catch-phrases into household words, from Mrs Mopp's "Can I do you now, Sir" to Colonel Chinstrap's "I don't mind if I do". Radio that winter also helped to warm the cockles of British hearts.

Christmas celebrations that year were somewhat muted. Christmas Eve was on a Sunday, still treated as the Sabbath, and then on Christmas Day we had a peasouper of a fog. I remember it well, for my brother-in-law had during the previous summer invested almost sixty pounds (a small fortune in those days) in a quite decent 10hp car. Petrol rationing having been in existence for almost three months, joy riding was very limited and, as he was keen to take his lady friend out on Boxing Day, he had to find a kind hearted soul with the necessary but unwanted coupons. Using someone else's coupons was strictly illegal, but I've yet to find anyone who could truthfully say that they never at some time during the war fiddled either petrol, food or clothing coupons. It became, unfortunately, almost a way of life.

I knew of a friend who I thought might be able to help my brother-in-law, rang him and was told yes, he did have four gallons to spare. This meant a trip from Romsey to Wilton and back, so bang went a gallon plus on that journey, not counting the three pints or so of household paraffin to eke out the precious petrol. The problem was that this unlawful dilution cut the car's performance to about fifty per cent — how we climbed steep hills I don't know. We started off. The weather was misty, but not too bad. As we progressed, it got steadily worse and when we reached Wilton we wasted no time before making the return journey, which became an absolute nightmare.

Fortunately there was little else on the road and fortunately indeed it was one of the last cars built with a running board, because I spent the whole time between Salisbury and Romsey outside the vehicle trying to find the verge.

The worst place was on the Romsey bypass, where by this time visibility was down to about three feet. I lost the kerb, we kept gingerly on. Then the car hit a bump and my brother-in-law stopped. I got down to investigate and found we had gone to the other side and were against the kerb some ten yards away from the road, at the entrance to Broadlands Estate! Somehow we got on our way and made the rest of the journey in safety — since then I've always been wary of fog.

Just after Christmas, I was busily engaged in churning out material for Style and Gerrish's winter sale. The public were warned "perhaps never again will such bargains be offered". These words were prophetic as it was their last sale and when peace returned most items (if obtainable) were about three times the price.

Chapter Fourteen 1940
Saved . . . by The Few

January was a very cold month and we found that fuel supplies were difficult to obtain. This situation persisted until rationing was introduced in the middle of the following year. Already we had rationing of butter, bacon and sugar, while meat was added in February. There was some murmuring because restaurant meals needed no coupons — a legitimate moan in the early days, but later on the establishment of British Restaurants offering meals at extremely moderate prices evened things up.

There was a further call-up, of twenty two-year-old men, in February and Salisbury almost came to a standstill on a Tuesday afternoon (market day) when thousands reported for enlistment (as requested) at the Salt Lane car park. For quite some time it was chaotic, then, with the aid of police, the area was cordoned off and the new recruits fell into ranks in many of the surrounding streets, then marched to the lorries waiting to take them to their destinations on Salisbury Plain. I expect the genius responsible for these stupid arrangements got a rocket, for the experiment was never repeated.

The Victoria Hall in Rollestone Street was now requisitioned and a Welsh regiment billeted there for a couple of months before they too made their way to France.

In March, I arrived home one evening to find a young staff sergeant from the Royal Army Service Corps sitting in the dining room. He wanted a billet and my wife had asked him to wait for me. In peacetime he had been assistant manager of one of the Commercial Bank of Scotland branches. We took to one another immediately and he stayed for seven weeks until being moved on. During that time, his fiancée came down from Wick in the North of Scotland and stayed for ten days. They were married in August and it was the start of a friendship that has now lasted over fifty years. I remember Peter showing me a copy of the *John o'Groat's Journal*, a small North of Scotland weekly newspaper that contained a classified advertisement which read: "While beachcombing at Wick in 1939, I came across an ancient vessel, which I think could be of Roman origin. It has a handle and the following inscription around the rim: *THI SI SAPIS POTAN DAT INO NE*. The translation has so far eluded me (my Latin is somewhat rusty). Could readers please help?" Peter thought this was hilarious and I am sure he was not unconnected with the ad's insertion.

The so-called phoney war suddenly came to an end, when on April 9th, the Germans invaded Denmark and Norway. Although our troops were sent to help the Norwegians, after successes around Narvik in the north, the enemy succeeded in advancing and our men had to withdraw. This, after Mr Chamberlain had told us "Hitler has missed the bus — our sea blockade is winning the war".

On May 10th, two days prior to Whit Sunday, Tom Singleton rushed into the street with the news that Hitler had invaded Holland and Belgium. The next weeks were a nightmare. First of all the papers fed us news of Allied successes. Then Rotterdam received the same treatment as Guernica — four days after the invasion the Dutch Army was ordered to lay down arms, the Belgian Army followed suit a fortnight later and by the end of the month, most of the British and French armies were cut off at Dunkirk.

Though that May was a nightmare, at long last this country woke up. Firstly and most importantly, Winston Churchill, who had for seven years been warning of the dangers inherent in Germany's arms build-up, became Prime Minister. Poor Mr Chamberlain, who was out of his depth as a wartime leader, did what he ought to have done in the previous September and stood down. By now he was a very sick man and he died a few months later. The papers were warning of the tricks used in the invasion of Holland. These included prior infiltration by so-called Fifth Columnists, parachutists who dropped in various guises such as members of the Dutch Army or Catholic priests — one story even mentioned nuns.

So it was with some relief that, on May 14th, we heard a speech over the radio by Mr Anthony Eden, the War Minister, who announced the setting up of a Home Defence Force, to be known as Local Defence Volunteers. Men not already engaged on military service and between the ages of seventeen and sixty five were eligible to join. We were told to enrol at our local police stations and within a few days the force was over a quarter of a million strong. I joined the Laverstock Platoon, which had twenty members that first week.

In the years since the war, we've been dubbed "Dad's Army" in a very derogatory sort of way. We were, or at any rate most of us were, raw amateurs but knowing what had happened in Holland and Belgium were prepared to do what we could to repel the expected parachutists. Our first parades were a shambles, but thanks to a few veterans from the First World War, we improved very quickly. Our patch was an area of some nine square miles. Our observation post, a shepherd's hut which a friendly farmer had hauled to the top of Laverstock Down, was in a splendid position, for we had a view of some fifteen miles to the north, south and west, although rather less to the east. Each night, six of us in turn made the two-mile trek to the top of the hill where the post was manned from dusk to dawn. The following night was free and the next night we manned a road block. The third night we were back on the down. Our uniform at that time simply consisted of a khaki armband bearing the letters LDV. This was not good enough for some platoons, who kept me busy making special ones giving the name of their village. One CO, a former brigadier, went one better and personalised his squad's armbands by adding a number, presumably in order that a body might be identified. Hitler ranted and raved about the new citizen army, warning that an armband could not be classed as a uniform and so we were all *francs-tireurs*, liable to be shot on sight, not being protected by International Law.

After about ten days, our weapons started to arrive. For several weeks we had one Lee-Enfield rifle from the First World War, three of the long-barrelled Canadian Ross rifles dating from the Boer War and twenty rounds of ammunition, five for each weapon. We were also loaned a double-barrelled shotgun and a .22 air rifle. These were augmented by a number of home-made weapons, put together in real country style — hoe and rake handles had carving knives, and even curved reap-hooks, spliced on to them, producing fearsome looking if not very practical weapons for use against a well trained army. At the end of June, half a dozen denim uniforms came through. We drew lots as the fairest method of distribution and I was lucky enough to get one. Without doubt those uniforms were ones rejected because no-one ever came of the required size which was six feet three inches tall, with a thirty six-inch chest and thirty two-inch waist. I was luckier than my colleagues as when five inches had been lopped off the legs mine was not a bad fit. After the first duty on the down I bought a pair of shiny black wellingtons, for the early morning dew made the grass pretty wet.

Another task we had was that of making Molotov cocktails. In an earlier chapter, I mentioned how a local man had volunteered to fight in the International Brigade in the Spanish Civil War. This chap — a First World War veteran — was now quite invaluable, for he put on a demonstration in a gravel pit at Alderbury and showed us how we could easily make these fire-bombs. A colleague and I went along to that Friday evening teach-in and for the next two weeks the whole platoon spent every available spare minute producing these weapons. We got bottles, filled them with a mixture of petrol and old engine oil in equal proportions, inserted a strip of cotton material about an inch wide by twelve inches long, left three inches of this outside the neck and bunged in the cork. When you needed to use the weapon, you pulled out the cork, lit the fuse and threw the "bomb" which broke on impact with solid objects. The mixture of old heavy oil and petrol was a deadly concoction and went on burning for up to ten minutes. Even one spot on a victim's clothes was enough to start an inferno.

Within a few weeks, sockets for tank traps appeared on entrances to each town and village in southern and eastern England. The traps themselves, made from old railway lines, were about twelve feet in length and bent to a right angle. Pill boxes appeared near the tank traps and railway bridges were strengthened to provide firing points. We were instructed in the best way to drop our home-made Molotov cocktails down the open hatches of tanks should they pass under the bridge. In retrospect it was all very amateur, but we at least felt that we were doing something. A few weeks later, wide and deep continuous tank-trap trenches were dug right across the country. In low lying land these quickly filled with water, which became stagnant and must have become a health hazard.

Quite soon, as the Allied position in France and Belgium became worse, an order was made resulting in the removal of all signposts for the duration, and for the obliteration of all place names including those used by traders, such as Salisbury Steam Laundry. In a way, this order when applied to Salisbury was quite ludicrous, while the Cathedral spire was still standing to tell the Germans which city they had reached. Most places possessed a landmark of some sort or another but I imagine this was an order made in a state of panic.

Winston Churchill's appointment was a breath of fresh air to the war effort, for he made Lord Beaverbrook Minister of Munitions and tough Ernie Bevin, the Union Leader, Minister of Labour. Shadow Spitfire factories appeared in the city, the premises of Wilts and Dorset Motor Company and Anna Valley Motors in Castle Street, being requisitioned for this purpose.

Towards the end of May, the news each day was ever more depressing. Then came the miracle of Dunkirk and many of the rescued troops came through the city. The voluntary services did a splendid job in supplying refreshments to the tired soldiers, day and night. The ordeal that the Army had suffered was plain for all to see. Almost without exception the men showed great fatigue. They had been unable to wash or shave for many days and most were minus items of uniform. On a Saturday evening I saw a distressing incident. A cheerful young Cockney wanting admission to the Assembly Rooms dance was refused as he was improperly dressed. True, the right leg of his uniform trousers had been ripped off just above the knee. Though it was difficult both for him and the doorman, he accepted the situation with a smile, unlike the retired officer who wrote to a National daily, complaining that surely the authorities could have at least re-kitted the returning troops prior to allowing them to be seen by the public. This attitude was not typical of most people, who did all they could to help the rescued army.

During June, a neighbour was a victim when the troopship *Lancastria* was torpedoed off the west coast of France, with the loss of nearly three thousand lives. Like many other hard-up HGV drivers, he had been attracted by the bounty offered to those who signed on for the Transport Reserve some eighteen months earlier. I remember one of his friends who also joined telling me "It's six quid a year for nothing — it's money for old rope".

On Monday, June 10th, Mussolini, who had been siting on the fence waiting to see how the battle would go, suddenly declared war on Britain and France. Though it was to prove to be his death warrant, at the time it was just one more nail in the Allies' coffin.

By this time, the worsening situation had made life on the home front very different. It was now essential to carry your identity card at all times, many members of the public were on the lookout for fifth columnists and many innocent people were interviewed by the police acting on hearsay.

My landlord, Jimmy Figgures, the secretary of the National Deposit Friendly Society, was especially vigilant. He was a small man, well versed in everyone's business, and one evening he was making his way home through St Edmund's Lane by the side of the churchyard. It was dusk, and through the gloom he saw some youngsters playing with rifles. As he watched, they lifted the lid on one of the square stone tombs and put the rifles inside. Jimmy went and had a look. He lifted the lid and, yes, there were the rifles. Off he marched to report to a friend, a police war reservist who returned with him to verify the truth of this arms cache. Now the pair went in the blackout to the Police Station, where the Chief Constable called in the Army. The lid was removed from the tomb and yes, there were indeed a number of rifles — all made of wood. The boys had been given them to play with. Originally, in the early years of the century, they had belonged to the Church Lads' Brigade, who used them for rifle drill. Poor old Jimmy, this escapade took some living down.

One member of Salisbury Chamber of Commerce did his bit in an effort to cheer people up. He distributed large cards which were to be seen in shops across the city Centre. They read: "There is no depression in this house. The possibilities of defeat do not exist. Queen Victoria."

The strange thing was that few people contemplated defeat, we felt that the country had muddled through on many occasions and without any doubt would do so again. By the middle of June we were standing alone, as France gave up the struggle. Winston Churchill's speeches were wonderful, especially his "We will fight them on the beaches" etc. This was just what the country needed at the time — it was only after the war was won we learned that as "Winnie" sat down after making that speech he murmured "but God knows what with".

In mid-June, in common with people all over England, I made an air raid shelter. This was for both my own family and my neighbour, whose husband, a retired RSM, had been commissioned and vanished back into the Army a year earlier. She had two children, then aged eleven and nine. The shelter, six feet square and six feet deep, was dug into solid chalk and lined with corrugated iron on a three by two-inch wooden framework. The centre of the roof, on which was some two or three feet of earth, was supported by a six-inch square post. I fixed wooden seats on two sides and a deck chair was placed against the other wall for my wife, who had to nurse our twenty-month old son. Before long, the shelter was in use quite often as the Luftwaffe began to raid towns on the coast and convoys passing through the Channel. After a while, my wife didn't bother to rush for cover during the day, but our Peggy, a tiny black spaniel, would make her own way to the shelter and then re-appear as soon as the all-clear sounded.

The Government now suggested that we organised our own fire-watching patrols on a street by street basis. We did this in our road without delay and quickly got well organised, with weekly charts showing when to report for duty. These were arranged so that they did not clash with LDV patrols and meant we had to be available one night in three, with three hours on and three off, but only during an air raid warning. Although the scheme was purely voluntary it worked remarkably well, with little dissension. It might easily have been otherwise for we often felt dog tired. The events of that summer engendered a truly remarkable spirit.

After a few weeks, we became accustomed to the new way of life. There was no longer the rushing about as soon as the siren sounded, which it often did even though enemy aircraft were perhaps fifty miles away. From our observation post we could watch searchlights in use at Southampton and Portsmouth and we also reported lights that were visible to us although not to air raid wardens in the city. We were especially worried at a flashing light that always made its appearance when the siren sounded and made a report. The Army sent a signals expert, who acknowledged himself quite baffled. It was certainly not Morse code. We were then loaned a theodolite and on the next occasion the siren went at night, we made a fix with the telescopic instrument and when dawn arrived, were able to pin-point the offending light. This proved to be a badly blacked-out roof light at the Modern School. It was above the stairwell and when the air raid warning sounded the masters and boarding pupils would rush through a swing door, which allowed light to penetrate. A simple explanation to a problem that was worrying at the time. We really thought we had a spy in our midst.

I had one of my so-called "free" evenings on a Monday at the end of June and went home to tea prior to returning to work in the constant endeavour to keep jobs up to date. During tea, I was so engrossed in the *Daily Mail* that I failed to watch the clock. I suddenly realised that it was ten minutes to seven, swallowed my drink and dashed for the bus back to Salisbury. When I opened the front door, I saw the double-decker pulling away from the bus stop only a hundred yards away. Possibly I swore under my breath, then started the walk of just over a mile.

As I descended Milford Hill on my way into the city, I saw the bus at the junction with Rampart Road, surrounded by a sizeable crowd. When I got to the scene, I discovered that there had been a violent collision. The bus had been going down the hill, the traffic lights changed from red to yellow and the driver of a car crossing the junction tried to beat the lights, with the result that his vehicle was almost flattened. Both occupants of the car were killed immediately. The driver, conductor and passengers on the bus were all taken to hospital with severe cuts and there was hardly a window that had not been shattered. At this time, as a non-smoker, it was a habit of mine to occupy one of the upstairs front seats when riding on a double-decker, so considered myself fortunate to have missed that bus. For the next few days I kept telling friends of my lucky escape, little knowing what Nemesis had in store.

In July, the sirens sounded more frequently and though there were no sustained raids, odd bombs were dropped along the coast and each incident provided its own rumours which grew with the telling. The army, which had left most of its equipment behind in France, now did a marvellous rush job in providing coastal defences. Steel scaffolding, which had made its appearance during the previous fifteen years, was requisitioned and I doubt if many realised just how much the country possessed, for it now stretched as defences all around the east and south coast. In vulnerable places even three lines of obstacles made from this most useful modern invention, reinforced with thousands of miles of barbed wire, showed the enemy that if he invaded it was not to be the picnic he had hitherto enjoyed.

In coastal resorts, camouflage artists really enjoyed life as they made newly erected pill boxes into ice-cream parlours or Tudor Tea Rooms. Thousands of concrete obstacles and dragons' teeth made their appearance both along the coast and inland at every possible route the Germans might take. It was staggering just how much was achieved in a few short weeks. How successful these defences might have been against a really determined enemy is another matter. It was the second miracle of organisation during that fateful summer, the first having been the rescue of three hundred-odd thousand troops from Dunkirk.

I remember during the second week of that month, I had a long conversation with Mr Robert Etchells, the Gaumont-British area manager, who worked from offices at Yeovil. He was somewhat shaken as on the previous day he had paid a visit to the Regent Cinema at Weymouth and just after his arrival the warning siren had sounded. The enemy made its first sustained attack on Portland and Weymouth. Mr Etchells had spent most of the day in a shelter and was now ready to recount the experience. It must have been fairly traumatic as almost two hundred lost their lives.

The night of July 15th/16th was the most memorable of my life. It followed a cloudy, wet day. That afternoon, a Monday, I was working on a display board for the Gaumont Palace, advertising the film *Each Dawn I Die*. It was still lying on the bench when I left for home, prior to going on duty. I can see it now — a sombre illustration of a gallows on a hilltop, against a dawn sky, the hangman's noose dangling loosely. I believe the star was James Cagney. I met the rest of my squad, or at least four of them, at about eight o'clock and off we trudged in wellingtons to our post about two miles away.

Among the four was a new recruit, an assistant in a Salisbury tailoring establishment. He had never even attended a drill session, but now he was given one of the long-barrelled Ross Rifles and his ration of five bullets. The sixth and absent member of the squad was a gormless seventeen-year-old named P---, not the brightest of boys by any means.

We reached our shepherd's hut and spent the next half hour chatting, then split into two parties for patrol until midnight. Three of my colleagues went off to the south, while I went to the north and east with Charlie Adlam, who had been a sergeant in the '14-18 war. It was a very quiet evening. From time to time we stopped in the gloom to watch a train coming down the Porton straight from London, listening to the changing sound as it braked to slow down and enter the tunnel outside Salisbury station and marvelling at the distance at which we could spot the sparks flying from the engine's chimney. From the air every engine must have been a wonderful target.

Towards midnight, we were patrolling the woods on the top of the down when we heard hesitating footsteps. I was nearest to the noise, so I challenged: "Halt, who goes there?" No answer. Again, "Halt, who goes there?" No answer. By this time, I had been joined by my colleague. I said: "Halt, or I fire." No answer. Charlie called: "Steady, Arthur, leave it to me." He went forward, rifle at the ready, and coming through the woods was the gormless idiot who should have been on duty at eight o'clock. Was I glad that my friend was an older and more experienced man, for otherwise I would possibly have killed a youngster and had to live with the knowledge for the rest of my life. True, I had gone correctly through the procedure and had every right to fire but he was after all, only a very stupid kid.

Shortly after this, Charlie and I were leaning over a gate, a mile from the hut and due east. We could see odd lights coming from the tented camp near Lopscombe Corner, some four miles away, where an Australian contingent originally bound for France had been living since arriving in this country. Their blackout precautions were appalling. It was a balmy night and we watched the searchlights at Southampton suddenly probe the sky, illuminating the barrage balloons. After a couple of minutes they were switched off — it was so peaceful. Suddenly there were five bright flashes, followed quickly by crump, crump, crump, crump, crump as small, high-explosive bombs fell about a mile from the camp, fortunately in open ground. Almost immediately we heard the engines of a plane. We guessed that the pilot had glided in from the coast, dropped his bombs and scarpered hell for leather. There was no air raid warning either before or after the bombing.

At midnight, three of our squad went to the hut to grab two hours' sleep before relieving Charlie, the new recruit and myself at two o'clock. The time passed without any more scares, except that on two occasions I had to warn H---, the new boy, about the way he was slinging his rifle. Instead of keeping the barrel tight against the back of his shoulder, it was at a forty-five degree angle. First he caught Charlie a glancing blow and then did the same to me.

I was looking forward to a kip and was glad when two o'clock came round. We made our way to the hut and wakened our comrades. After they had gone off on their patrol, we went in and, when we were all inside, shut the door. Because of the blackout, this was very necessary prior to lighting the candle lamp. Before Charlie could strike a match, I felt a terrific blow to my right forehead and saw a blinding light. H--- had come into the hut, still carrying his Ross rifle at an angle (we had left ours outside) and the barrel had struck me, breaking my glasses. The blinding light which I had experienced was when splintered glass went into my right eye.

Apparently the blow knocked me out and when I came to Charlie was trying to assess the damage by candlelight. He sent H---to find the others, and when they all came back it was decided that I must get to hospital. Don Adlam (Charlie's son, who was killed in Italy in 1944) came with me. I was in quite a bit of pain and the four-mile walk seemed to take an eternity.

On our arrival at the infirmary, a doctor took a quick look and decided that any action should wait until Mr Conroy Dixon, the local eye specialist, could be contacted in the morning. He bandaged my eye and instructed the nurse to get me off to bed in the Eye Ward, remove the pillows and put a sandbag on either side of my head. She drew the curtains and I undressed, put my uniform plus my shiny black wellingtons under the bed and hopped in. The nurse came back with the sandbags. It was all very quiet. I just lay there thinking that this sort of thing couldn't happen to me. It was most uncomfortable lying with my head absolutely flat and being unable to move it.

At about five thirty, the small ward began to come to life when a couple of probationers arrived for the morning wash. I lay there listening and heard a voice with a strong Wiltshire accent say "Yer mis, wot be he? A bloody Jerry? I bain't havin' that 'sno". She convinced him that I was as English as he was and constituted no threat. He told me later he had seen my boots under the bed — they were black so he thought flying boots, put two and two together and made five. He was a gamekeeper from near Mere, another LDV who had received a blast from a shotgun in the nether regions. Each afternoon, a doctor would arrive, give him a local anaesthetic in the backside and then proceed to take out about twenty tiny lead shot. The operation took a week and must have been most painful.

Mr Conroy Dixon, in response to an urgent call, arrived post-haste just after breakfast, took one look and told me that my right eye was now useless. After some thought, he said it would be best to try and leave it in as sometimes removing an eye upset the balance. It's difficult to describe my feelings at the news, I thought I would never be able to carry on my job — whoever heard of a one-eyed sign-writer? Over the next ten days everyone was very kind. My wife was chasing around and with the help of Mr George Howes, the New Picture House manager, found people to help out with my cinema contracts.

Unfortunately, the wound to the eye became septic and on Friday, July 26th, after I had passed a very painful night, Mr Dixon was again called early in the morning and decided to operate. He was most kind and apologised for the delay but hoped I understood his reasoning in not taking the eye out earlier. Of course I understood, but was pleased to go down to the theatre, as it would mean the end of most dreadful pain.

The following day I had an influx of visitors, sixteen in all. In two more days I was up. I went into the rest room, found a box of water-colours and set to, to see what I could do with my remaining eye. The ward sister came in and saw my lettering, and for the rest of my stay I had orders coming in daily from nurses wanting me to write nameplates for their doors.

For ten days after my admission I had had both eyes bandaged so could see nothing. It gave me an insight (hardly the right word) into the sixth sense which blind people seem to possess. My hearing became much more acute. For a couple of days a nurse had to feed me, then I tried to do it myself, quite successfully. One thing I did learn was never to judge a person's looks by their voice. One nurse, softly spoken and very kind, was quite wonderful. When she changed my dressings it was with a truly gentle touch. Another, with a hard voice and rough hands, did not feed me properly and I hated her near me. When I could see, I found the first was in her fifties and definitely behind the door when looks were given out, the other was, like me, in her mid-twenties and quite a raver — the sort men would fight over. All that glittered was definitely not gold — God help the man that married her! It is sometimes said that the blind are the best judges of character. After my experience I can well believe it.

The Battle of Britain had started on July 10th. By the time I left hospital on Sunday, August 4th, more air raids were a feature of life, although this area was fortunately not a target. I went along to meet the rest of the platoon on Monday evening and was chatting to a friend, then approaching sixty years of age, when suddenly he collapsed. Someone got hold of a car and rushed him to hospital, but when he was examined there was nothing physically wrong — just exhaustion and lack of sleep. There were many others who could possibly have gone to sleep on a clothes line but struggled on. By now, we were no longer LDV, we had become Home Guards. It sounded much more professional — another of Winnie's good ideas.

I well remember the afternoon of Thursday, August 8th when, although having been told to rest for a week, I went back to my workshop. There, just where I had left, it, was the display board for *Each Dawn I Die*. Wanting to see what I could do, I picked up my brushes and made a start, quickly realising that with only one eye writing would not be easy. During the first hour or so, I could have wept, for I could no longer judge the distance between my hand and the bench. I persevered, and within a few days had readjusted. After the initial problems, the loss of my eye has not been a handicap in my work — in fact, when getting down to really small lettering, it has been somewhat of an advantage. Today, as I approach my seventy seventh birthday, I am still able to manage lettering down to one eighth of an inch. However, even now if someone hands me a cup and saucer in mid-air, I always miss it by perhaps half an inch, but quickly correct the error, so that no-one ever seems to notice.

In the early days there were problems. I would bump into people, but soon adjusted and life went on as normal. The loss of that eye at the age of twenty five seemed like the end of the world, but I was lucky when compared to five of my school friends who gave their lives.

By the end of the month my black patch was redundant, for I was fitted with an artificial eye. At that time they were made of incredibly thin glass — the slightest drop and they were broken. Fortunately, Mr Conroy Dixon had done a wonderful job and retained the muscles so that I still possessed some movement. The first time that I wore the artificial eye on duty, P---, the gormless youngster I had nearly shot, said "Can you see alright with it?". When my son was small he always called it "Daddy's in-and-out eye".

On the afternoon of Wednesday, August 14th, I was waiting at the Infirmary to see Mr Conroy Dixon when the siren went. The nurses were dashing about, trying to find shelter for everyone. I left to make my way home, a distance of about a mile and a half. Dog fights were progressing high above the city; there was the constant rattle of machine guns and the cloudless sky was criss-crossed with vapour trails. The previous day, the Luftwaffe had a go at Andover, now they were after the Middle Wallop Fighter Station. Although some damage was caused, the attack failed. a Junkers 88 was shot down and crashed just inside the New Forest at Hale near Downton.

From now on aerial activity was constant as the Germans

endeavoured to knock out the Royal Air Forces' airfields. We were fed daily the number of enemy planes that had been claimed as shot down on the previous day — rather like a cricket score-board; that the claims were over-optimistic was to be proved after the war, but at the time it was good for morale.

On Saturday, August 31st, just as the pubs in the city were closing and the bus station filled with troops returning to camp, the air raid siren sounded. It was my free night and I was just about to go to bed when I heard the throb of what sounded like a German bomber, brrr, brrr, brrr. My wife and small son went down to the shelter while I remained in the garden, watching for any developments. The plane circled the city for several minutes and then made off. Shortly afterwards, several glows appeared from the eastern part of the city. Two of these grew rapidly and it was then obvious that Salisbury had received its first bombs. They were incendiaries — fifty of them.

Two major fires had started, one in Winchester Street at the Co-operative Society's men's outfitting department (I had worked on the first floor of the premises from 1931-1936) and one at Lindsey's builders yard and offices in Rollestone Street. Both premises were destroyed, but fortunately many other small fires were soon extinguished as the city was still crammed with people and help was quickly forthcoming. There was only one casualty — a resident of the Three Swans Yard, immediately behind the Co-op premises, thought he was trapped by the flames and suffered a slight stroke. He was taken to hospital but soon recovered. There is little doubt that the bus station had been the target, as most of the bombs fell within the area around.

During the next weekend, September 7th/8th, it seemed that Hitler was at last to make good his boast and invade. On the Saturday afternoon, the Luftwaffe made a concentrated raid on London using about seven hundred planes. We heard on the radio, with the BBC's usual understatement, that the enemy had succeeded in reaching London and fires had been started. Lord Haw-Haw, the mouthpiece of German radio, was for once much more accurate when he announced that the East End of London, was a sea of fire. As soon as darkness fell, more bombers arrived to stoke up the conflagration. As one member of the London Fire

"Never in the field of human conflict was so much owed by so many to so few."

The Prime Minister, Mr Winston Churchill,
House of Commons August 20th, 1940.

Went the day well?
He died and never knew.
But went the day
well or ill —
— England
he died for you.

"Aky's" memorial in the church-
yard at Holy Trinity, Warmwell,
Dorset. (See Page 32).

Service admitted to me, years later, "It was hell on earth and I was bloody scared".

I had hardly gone to bed before there was a knock on the window of our bungalow. On going to the door, I found it was our CO, a grand septuagenarian and retired Major-General. He told me to alert as many men as possible (six were already on the down, over two miles away) and report to the Command Post an hour before dawn. The code-word Cromwell had been received, so invasion was imminent.

None of us had much sleep that night. This was it — the real thing. Our Command Post was the tiny village hall, but as it had no phone, a small builder living almost opposite and possessing the only one within several hundred yards had been warned that in an emergency his sitting room-cum-office would be commandeered. Needless to say, when we knocked him up in the very early hours of Sunday morning we were far from popular, especially with his wife. She was one of those people who organised everyone and few possessed the courage to cross her.

With a colleague as runner, I took up position by the telephone. A warning was sent up to the squad on the down and the remaining dozen or so men settled in the village hall to wait for the call we thought would come at any moment telling us that the enemy had landed. There appeared to be an uncanny silence. We knew what had happened in Spain, Poland, Denmark, Holland and France, now it seemed it was our turn.

We waited ... and waited ... and waited. The only action came from the lady of the house, who was rather put out by the invasion of her domain so from time to time stuck her head round the door to see if we were still there. Not a single cup of tea was forthcoming during that long morning. The telephone remained silent — nothing stirred. It was just another peaceful Laverstock Sunday.

Suddenly that peace was shattered — the lady was in the doorway arrayed in Sunday best. She said: "Well, come on, Mr Maidment, time to stop playing soldiers, you'll have to clear out now, we're off to church." This struck me as ludicrous. There we were, waiting for parachutists to drop at any moment and she thought we were playing. I grinned and told her that we could not leave without an order from HQ. She almost exploded, her husband was ordered to go on without her, and she stayed to keep an eye on us.

At about three o'clock, the order came through to stand down. It was a false alarm owing to some clot misreading a signal and Jerry was not coming that day after all. In the event, he never did — just as well for at that time in 1940, we would have been no match for well trained paratroops.

Throughout the day, the Luftwaffe continued to rain bombs on London and the blitz went on almost without a pause. On Tuesday, September 10th, one of the Salisbury fire engines was dispatched with crew to Reading to take the place of one from the Berkshire town ordered as relief to London. By the middle of the week many fleeing from the East End arrived in Salisbury with horrendous tales of bombing.

In common with many other local people, my wife and I were only too pleased to give shelter to a couple of the refugees. Wartime Salisbury must have seemed heaven after their recent experiences.

Mr Ralph Ledra, the manager of the Gaumont Palace, even housed one family in a storeroom below the stage. This windowless dungeon-like place became their home for almost two years and during all that time the firm's area management were unaware of their presence.

The number killed in the capital during September reached seven thousand, with over nine thousand seriously injured.

Sunday, September 15th, was a day that gladdened all our hearts, for it seemed that our Hurricanes and Spitfires were bringing down the German raiders rather like pheasants at a country house shoot. Over the late evening news, the BBC told us that 185 enemy aircraft had been destroyed against RAF losses of only 25. Long after the end of hostilities, we learned that in fact only 61 German planes had been lost during that day against 31 British. Throughout the month, we were thrilled by the rapidly rising score of enemy aircraft shot down, on the 30th we were given the total of 1,097, our own losses 318. In reality the true figures were 629 and 358.

These unintentionally exaggerated claims did not give a completely untrue picture, for we were indeed winning the Battle of

Britain. Winston Churchill put our thoughts into words when he said "Never in the field of human conflict has so much been owed by so many to so few". It was thanks to the few that Hitler scrubbed his invasion plan, code-named Operation Sealion, for that year, and, as it transpired, for ever.

The nightly blitz by his bombers continued but Salisbury was fortunate and escaped this fate — but that's another story.